DIG ON FOR VICTORY

Dig On For Victory

Mr. Middleton's All-Year-Round Gardening Guide From 1945

C. H. Middleton

First published in this new edition
2009 by Aurum Press Ltd
7 Greenland Street
London NW1 0ND
www.aurumpress.co.uk

First published in 1945

A catalogue record for this book is available from the British Library.

ISBN 978 1 84513 499 0

3 5 7 9 10 8 6 4 2
2009 2011 2013 2012 2010

Printed in Great Britain by MPG Books, Bodmin, Cornwall

"Tell me, doctor..."

. . is it really true that a pin-prick could cause blood-poisoning?"

Whenever the skin is broken, however slightly, there is always a risk of infection. Against this constant menace modern science has provided a weapon — the modern antiseptic 'Dettol'.

To the germs that cause and spread septic infection 'Dettol' is a swift and ruthless killer. To you, and to the delicate tissue cells which the germs attack, it is just a clean, clear, non-poisonous fluid. Agreeable to use, pleasant to smell — it will not even stain linen, and yet germicidally it is three times more effective than pure carbolic acid.

Be on the safe side. Keep 'Dettol' always handy. On the cut or scratch that may fester, or when infectious illness threatens, use it promptly. Your doctor knows all about 'Dettol'.

FROM ALL CHEMISTS

DETTOL
THE MODERN ANTISEPTIC

Trade Mark

Conserve 'Dettol' for Medical and Surgical purposes. Do not use for sinks, drains, etc.

USE ROBBIALAC PAINTS

Greenhouses and potting frames have a funny knack of playing havoc with paint both inside and out. It is the **heat** and humidity that does it.

When you use paint for any kind of glasshouse it **must not only** stand up to heat and hard wear but possess **the ability to** contract and expand without flaking or breaking away.

White Robbialac Ready-Mixed Paint as an undercoating followed by Robbialac Hard Gloss Paint will impart a gleaming glossy-like surface on glasshouses—one that will remain white and **give** good service.

Remember that the Robbialac people make greenhouse paint for Horticulturists—what could be a better recommendation.

ON GREENHOUSES
POTTING FRAMES · GARDEN TOOLS · ETC

THE ROBBIALAC COMPANY. Proprietors: JENSON & NICHOLSON. LONDON. E.15.

MIDDLETON'S
ALL THE YEAR ROUND
GARDENING GUIDE
& ENCYCLOPÆDIA OF GARDENING

A detailed plan of work for every
week in the year & complete
A to Z Gardening Encyclopaedia

Edited by **C. H. MIDDLETON,**
Famous Broadcaster of the B.B.C.

Issued in Support of
THE MINISTRY OF AGRICULTURE'S
"DIG FOR VICTORY" CAMPAIGN

SHAW PUBLISHING CO., LTD.
6, CARMELITE ST , LONDON, E.C.4

HOW TO PRESERVE WOOD IN YOUR GARDEN

WITHOUT INJURY TO YOUR PLANTS

CUPRINOL is entirely different from any other wood preservative. The metallic salts in CUPRINOL do definitely preserve timber from rot and decay, and cannot be washed out by rain or damp.

FENCES AND GATES	Apply Brown U. (Cuprinol S.Q.D. Green if the wood has to be painted after treatment).
GLASSHOUSES	Where timber has to be painted after treatment — use Cuprinol S.Q.D. Green. If unpainted — use Standard Green.
FORCING FRAMES	Apply Standard Green Cuprinol with a brush. Leave it to dry before placing near growing plants.
SEED BOXES	Brush on Standard Green Cuprinol. It is harmless to plant life when dry.
BAMBOO CANES	Stand the ends in Standard Green Cuprinol, allowing the Cuprinol to penetrate the inside of the cane.

Specified and used by the Admiralty, War Office, Air Ministry, Home Office Ministry of Works & Planning, Public Authorities, Estates, Nurserymen.

CUPRINOL
WOOD AND FABRIC PRESERVATIVE
(Manufactured by Cuprinol Ltd., London)

Write to :
Jenson & Nicholson Ltd., Cuprinol Section, Jenson House, London, E.15

DISTRIBUTORS OF CUPRINOL PRODUCTS IN THE UNITED KINGDOM AND N. IRELAND

Mr. C. H. Middleton

introduces his

All the Year Round
GARDENING GUIDE

To My Gardening Friends :

This book is prompted by the numerous questions I have received from gardening friends all over the country. We have tried to work out the kind of book that would answer your questions in a simple and straightforward manner. I hope it will be of service to you. It is open for your comments and suggestions, so don't hesitate to let us know of any additions you would like in future editions.

That I have had a first-class collaborator is certain. Percy Dyer, N.D.H., D.I.P.A., has written most of the book. He knows his job, or he would not have been Superintendent of Parks at Farnworth, Lancashire, or have been able to make the splendid success he has of his wartime job as Air Ministry Horticultural Advisor for the Northern Region, controlling the production of so many thousands of acres at R.A.F. establishments that the censor will not let me say how many thousands.

So virtually this book brings Percy Dyer and myself into your garden as your fellow planners and growers. Here we try to make clear to you just what work we should want to do with you in every week of the year, if we were at your service with spade and fork and hoe and wheelbarrow.

Let me suggest a good gardening motto to hang up in your shed. Here it is :

" Plan your work ! Work your plan ! "

Here in this little book is the plan of work for every week from seed-time to harvest : and I wish you every success in working it.

C. H. Middleton

CONTENTS

		PAGE
Foreword by C. H. Middleton	... ...	7
How to Use This Guide	... ...	11
First Vital Stages in Garden Making	... ...	12
Cropping and Rotation Plan	... ...	50
Nine Rules for Bottling Fruit	... ...	126
Your Sowing and Planting Guide ...	... ...	130

WEEKLY WORK NOTES FOR ALL THE YEAR ROUND

		PAGE				PAGE
January	1st Week	15	July	1st Week	48
	2nd Week	16		2nd Week	49
	3rd Week	17		3rd Week	52
	4th Week	18		4th Week	53
February	1st Week	20	August	1st Week	54
	2nd Week	21		2nd Week	55
	3rd Week	22		3rd Week	56
	4th Week	23		4th Week	56
March	1st Week	25	September	1st Week	58
	2nd Week	27		2nd Week	59
	3rd Week	28		3rd Week	60
	4th Week	29		4th Week	61
	5th Week	30		5th Week	62
April	1st Week	33	October	1st Week	64
	2nd Week	34		2nd Week	65
	3rd Week	35		3rd Week	65
	4th Week	36		4th Week	67
May	1st Week	38	November	1st Week	68
	2nd Week	39		2nd Week	69
	3rd Week	40		3rd Week	70
	4th Week	41		4th Week	71
June	1st Week	42	December	1st Week	72
	2nd Week	43		2nd Week	73
	3rd Week	44		3rd Week	73
	4th Week	45		4th Week	74
	5th Week	46		5th Week	75

ENCYCLOPAEDIA of GARDENING from A to Z ... ... pages 77/129

The cartoon on the cover is one of Mr. Middleton's favourites.
It is reproduced here by courtesy of the " Daily Express."

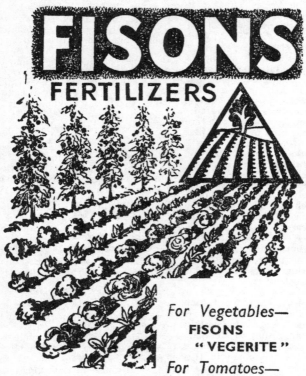

How to Use This Guide

MR. MIDDLETON has edited this book so as to make it a clear Guide to gardening work for every week in the year. Thus it is extremely easy to use and refer to. You just turn to the appropriate week of the year, and there you will find your programme of work clearly laid down.

In principle it is just as simple as that. But, as Mr. Middleton constantly reminds us, gardening needs common sense. You may need to glance over the notes for a few weeks before the current one, so as to get this week's programme into true perspective. Or, if you are taking over a rough or neglected plot rather late in the season, you will need to study also the notes on *First Vital Stages in Making Your Garden*.

Adapt for Special Cases

These are merely preliminary adaptations, after which the programmes of work will carry you expertly forward throughout the year.

The Week-by-Week Notes are fully representative, but, of course, not exhaustive. The many additional things which can be done depend on the extent of your gardening.

Notes for each week approximate as near as is possible to the correct time for each particular operation. It is obvious that the times for doing certain jobs must vary according to the part of the country you are in. Climate and conditions differ so much in this island of ours, and one season differs from another. It is not possible, therefore, to make hard-and-fast statements about anything to do with Nature. Nor can we draw any definite line between North and South, as some parts of Scotland are warmer and earlier than parts of southern England. The gardener should know something of his own local conditions, and regulate his work accordingly, sowing a week or two later than the normal time in very cold districts, and a little earlier in warm or sheltered localities.

How to Use the Encyclopaedia

Almost everything in Nature is seasonal, and all seasonal operations fall within the scope of the weekly notes. But some jobs may arise at any season. And even with items which involve seasonal operations, like growing cabbages, it is often convenient to be able to look up any one of them and to find everything about it in one place. That is where the *Encyclopædia of Gardening* comes in. Whatever you want to know about, there you will find it in its alphabetical position.

We have not hesitated to repeat when repetition has seemed useful. For instance, onion seeds can be sown any time from December to March, and in the weekly notes for this period the sowing of onions will be mentioned frequently. This will remind you to choose the best times for your one or two sowings.

Growing Under Glass

Work in glasshouses and frames is also dealt with, because the book seeks to serve you over the widest possible range. If you have neither glasshouse nor frame, aim to get at least a frame or a set of portable cloches as soon as possible. You will find this a sound investment as time goes on.

Occasional mention is made of such luxuries as fruit grown indoors, and outdoors on walls. This is for the benefit of those lucky enough to have such facilities.

Good Luck to Your Gardening

We believe that you will find this *Gardening Guide* a thoroughly good tool. When the time comes that we all feel free to scale down our utilitarian gardening, and we can think again of gardens of lawns and flowers, we hope to issue another edition of *Middleton's Gardening Guide*, leading the way back to the loveliness of gardens in a world at peace

FIRST VITAL STAGES IN

TWO things are demanded of a gardener: he must be interested, and he must be inquisitive. If you are both, you will not be satisfied until you get an answer to every question that arises; until you have discovered the cause behind every effect. And that is the way to profit by experience.

Whatever you do you will get results some good, some not so good, and by trial and error you will learn much.

You must also learn to use your own common sense, which is a gardener's greatest asset. To accept advice from others, and to adapt it to your own individual requirements and circumstances.

A Gardener is Judged by His Spade

Buy Good Tools.—The first thing after taking over a plot is to buy a spade. Do not borrow, buy. Choose a good one with an " all-bright " blade if you can find such a treasure. Look after it, keep it clean and sharp and it will last for years.

You can judge a gardener by his spade. The old-time gardener, like the old-time housewife, used to achieve miracles of brightness. Without going to those lengths, we can agree that clean, bright tools mean that the owner believes that a good tool deserves to be kept in good order. He knows, too, that dirt and rust mean friction, and friction means unnecessary physical labour.

Probably your new plot is covered with rough turf and weeds. How shall we begin? First remove all rubbish, such as bricks, pieces of timber and the like. Next divide the area into halves by putting a piece of string down the middle. Chop out some of the grass to mark the division, so that the string can be removed. Then skim off a strip of turf anything up to 2 ft. wide along the end of one half and lay it on the path opposite the end of the other

half. From then on dig as described in the notes on digging. (See *Encyclopædia*.)

Dig Wisely.—Now comes a word of warning. Do not break your neck over this digging. Digging is what you make it, a painful, back-aching ordeal, or a pleasant recreation, and if you are not used to it, it should be taken like medicine, in small doses. The beginner, full of enthusiasm, on the first good day in March or thereabouts, is apt to rush at it, and find it a lot harder than he imagined. Of course he soon tires, and ends with lumbago, and by calling his spade anything but a spade.

If ever you meet a man or woman who " can't bear gardening," it is a thousand to one that his or her keenness was burnt out in a series of wild rushes of that kind. Nature won't be rushed—neither human nature nor the good earth.

Now Draw Up Your Garden Plan

Draft Your Plan.—When the digging is proceeding, we can draw up our garden plan. A cosy fireside during a winter evening is a good time for this. Measure the outline of your garden as accurately as you can and make a small-scale drawing of it at, say, 1/10th in. to 1 ft. Note on it the points of the compass. Next study the cropping plan on pages 50/51, and decide which crops you wish to grow.

Now divide your garden into three main sections. One section you will allocate to green crops; one to root crops; and the third to peas, beans and miscellaneous crops. Some portions of your garden may be set aside for more permanent crops, such as rhubarb, herbs, etc. Having done this, mark on the plan, by means of lines, the positions you wish each particular vegetable to occupy. On page 180 is a table giving the distances apart at which vegetables should be sown or planted. Use this to

◀Mr. MIDDLETON says : *During wartime, step on the spade instead*

MAKING YOUR GARDEN

work out the distances on your plan, and mark it to scale.

Plan Your Crops.—Perhaps it may sound complicated and unnecessary to say " *Plan Your Crops*," but it is essential. Careful planning is the only way to make full use of land, to know exactly what crops we can grow, and to calculate how many seeds or plants we need to buy. By doing it we shall avoid the common mistake of putting in seeds and plants at odd times when we happen to buy them, and ending with a hotch-potch of crops which somehow does not supply anything we want. It is only too easy to fill a garden, and then find suddenly that there is no room left for half the things we intended to grow.

Your plot may not be a perfect shape such as the cropping plan given on pages 50/51 illustrates, but no matter what its shape, it does not require much ingenuity to plan a crop lay-out. Remember that as a general rule rows are better running north to south. They need not, however, be exactly north to south, but it is better if they can get the benefit of sunshine on both sides.

It is a convenience to set aside a small portion of your ground as a seed bed to enable you to raise plants in advance for planting out in their permanent quarters as the ground becomes ready for them.

Art of Growing from Seed

Having prepared your plan, you should finish the digging, which should, wherever possible, be done before Christmas, to allow frost and snow to penetrate the soil. Calculate your seed and plant requirements, and order them early.

Your Seed Bed.—All members of the cabbage family, such as Brussels sprouts, kale, sprouting broccoli ; and other crops such as leeks, are usually, for convenience sake, sown on a seed bed and later transferred to their permanent positions. The piece of land chosen for this purpose should be in good heart, but need not have too rich a soil, as it is better to transplant from poorer to richer soil, not the other way round, starting the plants, like babies, on a light diet and putting them on stronger food as they grow up. The seed bed need not be large ; for a small garden an area 6 ft. by 4 ft. would be adequate.

The soil should be well prepared. In early spring, on a suitable day when the ground is reasonably dry and does not stick to your boots, the soil should be

(*continued overleaf*)

Reward
of
Good
Gardening

of the accelerator. You'll reach your journey's end quicker. ▶

forked through. If it had been dug during the winter it will break down into a very fine tilth. Forking will level the surface. Before any seeds are sown the whole should be well trodden. This is done by standing with the feet together at the edge of the piece, then moving them a few inches to the side at a time. As each foot is moved the weight of the body is brought on to it. You just walk sideways, taking very short steps. Cover the whole bed in this way to firm it. Then rake down the surface, giving it a fine finish, and remove hard lumps, sticks and stones.

Raking requires considerable skill to do well, and is worth practising. Any portion of the garden where seeds are to be sown, in addition to the seed bed, should be prepared in this way. Judgment must be exercised as to whether or not treading will be necessary. If your soil is light and sandy, or is old garden soil which has been worked for many years, then the above treatment is essential. If the spring has been very dry, then almost all soils will need to be firmed. But where soils are heavy, and in the wetter parts of the country, treading should be omitted. Raking down will be sufficient.

Seed Sowing.—On the seed bed, drills can be made by merely laying a stick on the soil and pushing it down so that it makes a mark half an inch deep. If it is a large seed bed it will be necessary to draw the drills with a hoe, using a line as a guide. Make the drills nine inches to a foot apart, to allow for hoeing, and sow the seeds very thinly. Rake the soil over them and mark the position of the drill with a label at one end and a short stick at the other. It pays to get good wooden labels and to mark everything in the garden. A record should be kept of names of varieties, the merchants who supplied the seed, and date of sowing or planting, and subsequent results.

In the weekly notes in the following pages, reference is occasionally made to the sowing of seeds *broadcast*. This means scattering the seeds over a patch

of soil or in a frame instead of sowing in drills. It is a useful method with early carrots and radishes. The soil is raked fine, and the seeds are sprinkled on it very thinly. They are then covered by sieving and dusting fine, sandy soil over them. This is the way to hold the seeds down and prevent them being washed together into clusters by rain or by watering.

In the open garden seeds are usually sown in drills made with a hoe. You should use a line or string drawn tight as a guide. Stand on the line as you work, to prevent it being moved out of the straight. Walk backwards as you pull out the soil. V-shaped drills can be drawn either with a special triangular hoe or with a corner of the ordinary hoe. Flat drills are taken out with the hoe to the required depth, the soil being pulled to the side. After sowing, replace the soil with the rake, using the back of it for shallow drills. When raking, work in the reverse direction to that followed when making the drill. A final very light raking gives the bed a good finish and removes footprints.

Soil, Seeds and Drills.—The depth of drills varies according to the vegetable and the soil. Seeds like onions and leeks are sown in drills as shallow as it is possible to make them. Small-seeded varieties such as carrots, turnips, all the cabbage family, radishes, and parsnips, are sown $\frac{1}{2}$-in. deep, while larger seeds are sown more deeply. The depth of drills for peas and beans, artichokes and potatoes varies according to the soil. The lighter the soil the deeper they are sown, the heavier the soil the more shallow the drill.

A final point. On light soils and in dry seasons it sometimes pays to water the drills before sowing the seed. Allow a few hours to elapse before sowing to permit excess water to drain away.

———

Now we are ready for plans in greater detail. Each week through the seasons brings its special tasks, and these are discussed fully in the following pages.

◀ **Mr. MIDDLETON** says : *Digging is what you make it—a*

GARDENING GUIDE *for* EVERY WEEK
ALL THE YEAR ROUND

JANUARY

JANUARY—1st WEEK

1. Prepare Your Cropping Plan.—Draw up your cropping plan without delay for the coming season. If you are a beginner it will be straightforward work requiring only a measured outline of the garden drawn to scale, on which the future position of crops can be marked (see cropping plan and rotation of crops, pages 50 and 51).

Old hands will take into consideration what they have grown in the past and where they have grown it. They will also take account of their successes and failures, and adjust plans accordingly.

Some gardeners, wiser than the rest, keep a notebook record of what they do in the garden, the results they get, and how things went wrong. Thus, by not relying on memory alone they make the most of their experience. This habit is commended to all.

The most important rule in planning a vegetable garden layout is to " rotate the crops " ; in other words, to grow each vegetable in a place different from that occupied by it last year. The only possible exception to this is the onion, which will often succeed quite well on the same ground for several years. But there is no real advantage in this, and it is usually more convenient to work the onions into the rotation scheme, provided, of course, they can always be given rich, deep soil.

2. Order Seeds and Seed Potatoes.—Having planned the garden, order your seeds. To help you in calculating the amounts required, you will find a table of seed quantities on page 130. Early ordering helps the seedsman as well as yourself. Do not let things slide, get most of your requirements at once, and avoid this business of piecemeal purchasing of odd packets of seeds. Seed potatoes should also be obtained early so that you may sprout them. This particularly applies to early varieties.

3. Dig when Possible.—All these jobs can be done when the weather is bad. On good days, if the soil is in reasonable condition, we must dig. Few gardeners complete this foundation work before Christmas, though it is better to do so. The wise gardener's digging motto should be *little and often*. As land is cleared of standing crops, such as celery, leeks and parsnips, turn over the soil and add manure. Also prepare now any additional land which may be available.

4. Force Rhubarb Indoors.—Rhubarb forcing, which you will have begun earlier, should be continued, lifting roots as necessary and bringing them into a greenhouse. Place the roots under a bench, and keep them in the dark. Pack each root well with soil and keep moist. Before bringing inside, the roots should be lifted out of the soil and left on the surface for at least a week, exposed to the weather.

5. Sow Onions and Lettuce in Greenhouse.—Onions and lettuce can now be

pleasant, healthy recreation, or a painful ordeal   *Hasten slowly.* ▶

sown in boxes in heat. This is essential for onions if you want to grow large bulbs. The soil used should be light and well mixed, and pressed firmly into the boxes. Either broadcast the seeds over the surface or space them out one inch apart. This latter method obviates pricking out, but should only be done with reliable seed. Choose only large variety onions for this sowing, e.g. *Ailsa Craig*, *Premier*, *Cranston's Excelsior*, and other well-recommended varieties.

6. Finish Pruning Fruit, and Spray. —In the fruit garden, carry on with pruning. Spraying apparatus should be thoroughly overhauled before applying winter insecticidal washes. Winter-spray fruit trees.

JANUARY—2nd WEEK

1. Manure and Lime: More Digging.—Digging should go forward steadily when possible. It is a good idea to ridge the land so as to expose a large surface to the pulverising action of the weather. Incorporate manure or rotted compost material where desired.

Lime may be applied in the form known as hydrated lime. It is particularly suitable for dressing now or later on land dug and manured in late autumn. Manure and lime should never be applied at the same time, as chemical action of the lime releases valuable properties from the manure in the form of gas. On heavy soils it is usually better to dig-in manure before Christmas, and unless you are satisfied that the soil already contains sufficient, apply lime in the spring. On light, sandy soil the other way round is better, because the winter rains might wash away much of the goodness of the manure. Lime should be applied at half-pound per square yard and forked lightly into the surface. Do not leave it on top, or bury it too deep.

2. Onions and Cauliflowers.—Make another sowing of onions indoors to raise plants for putting out in May.

Sow a few cauliflowers in a box in warmth, to give plants for putting out in April. Choose a variety such as *Early Erfurt*, and keep them in cooler conditions when germinated. Some of you may have made a September sowing and will now have good hardy plants in a cold frame. Examine occasionally, ward off slug attacks, and give air when weather permits.

Autumn-sown onions in the open garden may need protection in the colder and more exposed parts of the country. An improvised frame can be erected over them, or cloches can be used.

3. Water Lettuces.—Lettuce growing in the greenhouse borders, having been planted there after the tomatoes were cleared, will need careful handing. They should not be stinted of water, but it should be applied in such a way as to prevent drops getting on the leaves. Plants which " flag " or wilt rarely recover. Remove any leaves which turn brown and die. Make another sowing inside to raise plants to follow these. Choose a variety such as *Cheshunt Early Giant*, *Arctic King* or *May Queen*.

4. Sow Peas in Pots.—Peas may be sown one or two seeds in a small pot, or 3 in. apart in boxes, and kept in cold frame to be planted out in March and early April. This is a method more suited to the southern or mild districts where good growing conditions arrive earlier than is usual in the north. It is much preferred by some growers to the very early sowings in the open border.

5. Examine Potatoes, etc., in Store.— Look through the potato clamps and pick out any tubers which are rotten or going bad. This prevents the spread of decay through the clamp.

Other root crops in store such as carrots, turnips, and beetroot should also be examined for decay and bad ones thrown out. The others should then be re-stored. Onions, which are kept in a cool airy room, should be gone over regularly for bad specimens. Any showing signs of decay should be

◀ Mr. MIDDLETON says : *An allotment is rather like the army.*

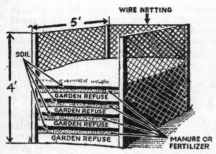

Simple compost heap built in layers, for good air penetration. Another method is shown on page 66.

destroyed, or used immediately. If you intend to save your own onion seed, pick out a good specimen or two and pot them into a 7-in. pot. Shallots saved for planting should also be regularly examined. Those with mould on them, or which are soft and decayed, should be thrown out. Only good, firm bulbs must be kept for this purpose.

6. Prune Fruit Trees.—Winter fruit-tree pruning should go on apace. Large standard and half-standard specimens will require no pruning apart from removal of any dead wood, and an occasional thinning of the branches where overcrowded. Other forms such as bush, pyramid and cordons will need more attention in this respect. All pruning should be done before spraying begins, to avoid wastage of material. (See *Pruning*.)

7. Winter Spraying.—Spraying should be done as soon as possible. The purpose of winter spraying is to destroy hibernating pests, the eggs of insects laid on the branches and twigs. It is essential if good quality, clean fruit is to be obtained. The usual spray employed is a tar-distillate wash. A newer spray which is said to be more effective is now also in use. It is known as *D.N.C.* (*Dinitro-O-Cresol*), and is obtainable under various proprietary names. It is more effective against capsid bug than tar-distillate. Full

directions for use are usually given on the containers. Apples and pears should be left until the last, first completing apricots, cherries, peaches, plums, and the bush fruits such as currants and gooseberries. Spray also deciduous hedges such as quickthorn, but keep the fluid away from evergreens, or green vegetables, or it will burn the leaves.

JANUARY—3rd WEEK

1. Dig, and Clean Up.—Before you complete your digging, thoroughly clean all around your garden. Brush down the fences and walls, rake out all dead leaves and rubbish from hedge bottoms, scrape and clean all paths, and trim grass verges. Some of the rubbish will have to be burnt, and it will produce useful wood ash, which should be kept dry for future use. Other softer material can be buried in the trenches while digging. The reason for this cleaning is not only to tidy the garden, but to destroy as many as possible of the insect pests which will be hibernating on walls, fences, and in hedges.

2. Prepare More Forced Rhubarb.—Keep up a succession of rhubarb " crowns " lifted from outside for a steady supply of forced sticks.

3. Force Seakale.—Begin to force seakale crowns outside by placing a good box (about 18 in. deep), a special seakale pot, or a small barrel, over selected ones, and keep over this a foot thickness of fresh stable manure to produce heat. Fairly fresh leaves are quite good if manure is not available. Crowns may be lifted and forced inside. Place them a few inches apart in large pots or boxes of soil, and put under a bench in a greenhouse or in a shed. Keep dark and in a temperature of 45° to 50° F.

4. Sow Onions and Lettuce.—Sow onions inside if necessary. Sow lettuce for succession, if desired. Varieties such as *May King* or *Golden Ball* are ideal for culture in cold frames or under cloches.

The first month is the worst : after that you begin to enjoy it. ▶

5. First Sowing of Tomatoes.—The first real sowing of tomatoes can be made now. These plants should produce fruit in June. In the northern or colder parts of the country, particularly in industrial areas, it is not wise to attempt to produce fruit earlier than this. Seeds sown before or about Christmas produce only weak plants, as the light is not strong enough to give sturdiness. Gardeners in the north who wish to produce early fruit should buy in February good, strong plants raised in the south of England.

6. Force Herbs.—It is well worth while to force a few herbs, particularly where onions are scarce, as they are invaluable for flavouring. Mint, chives and tarragon are especially suited to this treatment. Lift a few roots from outside and place in boxes of soil in a temperature of about 55° F.

7. Examine Seed Potatoes.—Seed potatoes of early varieties, as soon as obtained, should be set up in single layers in shallow boxes. The " rose " end, which is the end containing the " eyes," should be placed upwards to permit proper sprouting. Any inadvertently put the wrong way should be reversed as soon as noticed. Place the boxes in a cold room or greenhouse in plenty of light. Allow adequate ventilation, but keep frost out.

8. Spraying and Pruning Fruit Trees. —In the fruit garden, carry on with pruning and spraying as conditions permit. Spraying can be done only on still days. Wind is wasteful of spray liquid and may cause damage to the laundry next door. Therefore prune when windy, spray when still. Mix up only enough liquid for the particular period so that it can be used immediately. It should never be allowed to stand, and should always be fresh. Make sure good cover has been given to all twigs and branches. If Red Spider Mite has been troublesome, a little petroleum spray such as *Winter Volck* should be added to the tar-distillate wash (about 1 per cent.). This is more destructive of the eggs, as it is also of capsid bug eggs, which are laid deep in the bark and have only a small cap exposed to the air.

9. After a Gale.—After any gale examine all trees for loose stakes and broken bands. This is particularly necessary with young ones planted in early winter. They may be loosened in the soil and must be firmed again. Established trees sometimes die from being loosened at the root, so the same applies to them.

JANUARY—4th WEEK

1. Start New Compost Heap.—When bad weather prevents a continuance of digging, repairs can be made to path edgings where necessary. A certain amount is always required with tiles, bricks or wood. Path surfaces may also need attention.

The old compost heap having been dug into the ground during digging operations, a start should now be made in building a new one. Little will be available at present apart from leaves, but every little helps, and all house-refuse of a decayable nature which is of no use for food for man or beast, should be added to it.

2. Sow Cauliflowers.—A box of cauliflower seeds, *Early Erfurt* or *Early London*, can be sown to provide plants for growing on in frames, or cold greenhouse, or in the open. They are very suitable for planting after lettuce in frames or greenhouse. In the greenhouse they will mature in time for the planting of tomatoes.

3. Sow Mustard and Cress.—In the warm greenhouse, mustard and cress can be grown in boxes or on a soil border. For a small family a box of each is usually enough to provide salads for a week to a fortnight. Fortnightly sowings can be made all through the winter, putting in the cress three or four days before the mustard, because it takes longer to germinate. Just press the seed gently into the soil with a flat piece of wood, water it, and cover with paper until germinated.

◀ Mr. MIDDLETON says: *Keep your tools clean and*

4. Prick Out Seedlings.—If necessary further sowings of lettuce can be made. Seedlings of these and onions from early sowings must be pricked out as ready. Handle lettuce carefully, and do not bruise the leaves. Onions also need careful treatment and should not be buried too deep, nor so shallow that they fall over. Sown thinly they may not need pricking out. Those boxes in which the seeds were spaced out may have a number of blanks where seeds have failed. Fill these up from one of the boxes. Onions for exhibition are pricked out into small pots. Water carefully when finished.

5. Examine Cabbage, Kale and Broccoli.—In the open garden a steady supply of greens should be available. The cabbage *January King* is now coming along, and given favourable weather will last for weeks. Savoys and kales will also be available. See that nothing is wasted. In the north the kales and broccoli often take on a depressing appearance at this time of year, but later, new shoots will be produced which will be very valuable. Bend over the leaves of broccoli to protect centres against frost.

6. Protect Plants in Frames Against Frost.—Cold frames containing plants will need special protection during severe weather, but see that they have plenty of ventilation when possible. Whenever frost threatens, cloths and mats must be put over the lights, or straw and bracken can be used. Mats or sacks are best because they last for a long time, whereas straw or bracken are short-lived. Cloches covering crops out of doors will need frequent attention, as they get out of alignment and so their protective power is weakened. Both ends of a row of cloches should be blocked with glass to prevent draughts. Remove dead or diseased leaves.

7. Protect Broad Beans and Spring Cabbage.—Broad beans sown in November should have soil drawn up to them as a protection. If the weather permits and the soil is in suitable condition, another sowing can be made. These plants often catch up with those put in earlier. January sowings are normally possible only in the southern parts of the country or in well-protected gardens. In the north they can only be made in the mildest of winters. Spring cabbage should be protected by drawing the soil up to the stems. This encourages new roots from the stems which give greater support and better anchorage.

8. Lift and Store Artichokes.—Jerusalem artichokes can, if convenient, be left in the soil and dug up as required for use, but it is really better to lift them all now and clean the land thoroughly and dig it. The tubers can be stored, and those suitable for replanting picked out. Egg-size is normally regarded as best for this purpose. If left in the land they grow wild and become unmanageable, and are thus better replanted annually.

9. Fruit in Store.—Apples and pears in the store-room will now need going through regularly. Those showing signs of decay should be destroyed. Others beginning to shrink and wrinkle should be put to immediate use. Good, sound fruit which will keep for some time are better spaced out thinly, not in contact with each other. Use late pears as soon as they begin to soften, because the process of decay follows immediately on that of ripening.

10. Fruit - Tree Pruning.—Before spraying old espalier-trained fruit-trees, it is sometimes better to thin out the fruit spurs. Trees can carry too many spurs. They produce masses of blossoms and few fruits. In extreme cases every alternate spur could be cut away.

11. Start Hot-House Fruit.—Inside fruit, such as vines, can be started. The pruning will have been completed and the rods left hanging horizontally. This helps even bud-development when heat is turned into the house. Ventilation must be well controlled. To start peaches the ventilators of the greenhouse should be closed, and a temperature of 45°–50° F. maintained.

bright. No man can dig properly with a dirty spade. ▶

FEBRUARY—1st WEEK

1. How to Use Bad Weather.—February is noted for its wetness. If it lives up to its reputation, work in the garden is at a standstill. Much can be done in the greenhouse, however. Frames and outdoor crops will need protection in severe weather. Parsnips can be lifted and stored in wet sand, thus clearing the soil for digging. Similarly leeks can be moved and heeled together in a frame or protected corner.

2. Plant Shallots.—Where weather conditions permit, shallots can be planted. Thoroughly prepare the bed, dressing it with a good general fertilizer, a little extra superphosphate of lime or bone meal, and some wood ash. Rake or fork this in. Plant only good sound bulbs in rows 12 in. apart. In dealing with shallots, push the bulbs half into the soil 9 in. apart.

3. Plant Artichokes.—Plant artichokes as soon as conditions permit. Minimum distances apart are 12 in. between the tubers and 30 in. between rows. For the ordinary garden, one row is usually adequate, and this is placed where these tall plants will not shade other crops but will give some protection against winds. Plant good tubers in V-shaped drills 5 to 6 in. deep.

4. Fill up Spring-Cabbage Rows.—Spring cabbage may have suffered severely if the winter has been severe or very wet and cold. It is a good idea to keep some plants in a frame protected with lights in bad weather, and use these to fill the blanks. In emergency seeds can be sown inside in 50° F., and the plants grown on quickly for this purpose. In most parts of the north this crop is a doubtful proposition, though in some favoured spots it is often successful. As soon as the worst weather is past, stimulate the plants with a dressing of nitrate of soda, hoed in between the rows.

5. Sow Maincrop Onions.—Maincrop onions, varieties such as *Bedfordshire Champion* or *James Keeping*, can now be sown indoors to give plants for putting out in May. This method is essential in such parts of the country as Lancashire, where it is not normally possible to sow outside in March early enough to give good results. Leeks should be sown inside also, in the greenhouse or in a warm frame. In rows 9 in. apart a large number can be raised, and this sowing gives large plants for early planting. Here, again, it is necessary in the north where June planting is essential.

6. Sow Sprouts and Cucumbers.—Brussels sprouts require a long season of growth, and plants of the earliest crops are raised from seeds sown now in a frame. They can be sown in boxes and pricked out into a frame if desired.

Cucumbers for fruiting in early summer are sown now. Place the seeds singly in small pots, pushing them in sideways, not laying them flat. Cucumber seeds are large and ovoid in shape. Keep in a temperature of 55° to 60° F. Seedlings in the greenhouse should be kept as near to the glass as possible to prevent them being "drawn." Prick out seedling tomatoes when 2-in. high and the seed-leaves are well developed.

7. Examine Seed Potatoes.—Seed potatoes which are sprouting can be

◀ **Mr. MIDDLETON** says : *Take digging easy at first, or you may*

examined, and the number of sprouts reduced; the more sprouts you leave the more small potatoes you will get. With less sprouts the tubers will be fewer but larger. So for main crops not more than two should be left; more for earlies if you prefer plenty of small new potatoes. Any showing very elongated sprouts are probably diseased and must be destroyed.

8. Prune New Fruit Trees.—Fruit trees planted in early winter should have produced some root growth and will now be able to stand pruning. This early pruning is mainly to form a framework and to train the tree. Small bush apples and pears may be purchased already trained, and will need only light pruning. Trees bought now for planting will have been pruned by the nurseryman. Tree fruits and soft fruits can be planted now if the soil is in good condition. It must not be done if the weather is wet and the soil pasty. The strawberry bed can be prepared for planting. August is the best planting month for strawberries, but plants can be put in during late winter. They must not be allowed to bear fruit, however, during their first season, whereas those planted during autumn can carry a crop.

9. Feed Wall Fruits.—Wall fruits having been pruned and sprayed should have an inch or so of the soil scraped from the border and replaced with good loam. Bone meal and general fertilizer can be mixed with the loam, and for stone fruits some hydrated lime.

FEBRUARY—2nd WEEK

1. Sow Peas, Radish, Spinach, Parsnips, Broad Beans.—In the southern parts of the country in sheltered areas a beginning can be made with some early outside seed-sowings. In a warm position sow peas, radish and round-seeded spinach. In the open garden sow parsnips and broad beans as soon as the soil can be worked without caking and making your boots muddy. In cold districts further north none of these sowings will be possible until later.

Broad beans can be set in boxes and grown on in a frame to be planted out as soon as conditions improve.

2. Make and Begin to Use Hot-Bed.—Make up a hot-bed of fresh stable manure and leaves, 2 ft. deep, cover with a 6-in. layer of good soil and put over a wooden frame and light. (See *Hot-Bed*.) Sow turnips, radishes, carrots and cabbages in this soil.

3. Forcing Rhubarb and Seakale Outside.—Rhubarb and seakale can be forced outside, more slowly than indoors, but will provide sticks to follow the earlier crops. Deep boxes or barrels placed over the crowns and covered with a good layer of warm manure, or fermenting leaves will encourage growth.

4. Prepare Onions for Transplanting.—Onions such as *Giant Rocca* or *Giant Zittau*, sown out of doors in autumn, should be hoed between the rows preparatory to planting out as soon as conditions permit. Those covered with cloches, or temporary frames and lights, need plenty of air whenever possible. As soon as the worst of the weather is over remove these protections.

5. Sow Summer Cabbage and Cauliflowers.—Sow early summer cabbages and red cabbages in a frame. The red cabbages will provide a crop in July and August. Do not grow many of these unless you like them cooked as well as pickled. If seedlings of cauliflowers are wanted for a succession, make another small sowing.

6. Pot Young Tomatoes.—Young tomatoes from a January sowing, if well established and about 3-in. high, should be potted into 3½-in. pots, using a good mixture of loam, peat or leaf mould and sand, with a little fertilizer added. Keep in a temperature of about 60° F. A successional crop may be needed, and a further sowing can be made. Good varieties are *Best of All, Market King, Stoners M.P., Ailsa Craig*.

7. Protect Wall - Fruit Blossom.—Wall fruits, such as peaches, will be coming into flower. This blossom must

get blisters and lumbago, and call the spade anything but a spade. ▶

be protected from frost. Fish nets doubled are usually employed, while tiffany is quite useful. The cover should be draped in such a way as not to rest on the trees. Peaches and nectarines are prone to a serious disease known as Peach-Leaf-Curl. It causes the leaves to become corrugated and blistered, and in serious cases all the leaves fall off. Attacked leaves should be burned. To control the disease, spray the trees with Bordeaux or Burgundy mixture just before the buds open, when the spores are most vulnerable.

8. Complete Fruit-Planting.—Where fruit-planting was not completed in early winter it can be done now if soil conditions allow. If it cannot be done, all trees should be heeled in and their roots well covered with soil until they can be dealt with.

9. Cut Back New Raspberries.— Raspberries planted in autumn can now be cut back to 12 in. from the ground. The canes are first allowed to establish themselves before being cut in this way. It is always a temptation to allow the cane to stay as it is, in the hopes of getting some fruit the first year. This is a great mistake. The fruit is invariably poor and subsequent growths are produced high up the stem instead of at ground level. Growths to fruit the following year are wanted, and these must arise at the base. Raspberries can be planted any time during the winter, but the earlier the better. If planted after Christmas, allow some weeks to pass before cutting back.

10. Protect Fruit Buds.—Bush fruits and wall fruits are frequently attacked by birds, particularly bullfinches, which destroy the buds. Black cotton intertwined amongst the branches will help to scare them away.

FEBRUARY—3rd WEEK

1. Sow and Transplant Onions.— Onions sown in January should be pricked out as soon as possible. The sowing of maincrop varieties should be made without delay. In the south, if the soil is in workable condition and the weather good, we can transplant onions sown outside in autumn. Choose a well-prepared and sheltered position

2. Making New Rhubarb Bed.—A new bed of rhubarb can be made now either by buying crowns and planting them, or by lifting good, healthy roots from an existing bed and splitting them into portions. Each portion must have a terminal bud. Prepare the soil well by deep digging and incorporating as much manure as can be spared. Plant 3 to 4 ft. apart. Such new beds should be made up periodically to replace roots lifted for forcing. Forced roots can be replanted, but take a few years to recover.

3. Fill Up and Hoe Cabbage Rows.— As the weather improves hoe between spring cabbage, first giving a dressing of stimulating fertilizer. Fill any blanks either from a frame or by using up one of the rows. Prepare the onion bed as soon as possible. Its position will have been fixed in the cropping plan, and the experienced gardener will have given it preferential treatment in the way of manure. Dress on bone meal at the rate of four ounces per square yard. Lime can be put on now also, and if desired, a little old soot (fresh soot is dangerous), while wood ash is very valuable. All this should be well forked in and a good tilth produced on the bed. General fertilizer can be applied just before planting or sowing.

4. Examine Broccoli.—Heading broccoli, which will mature from March to May, should be examined occasionally and have dead leaves removed. Probably you will have heeled them over to the north to avoid frost damage. In the south a succession of heads can be had right through the winter by skilful seed sowing and using a wide range of varieties. In the north those varieties which mature from January to March are rarely successful.

Shallots, if not already in, should be planted as soon as the soil is in workable condition. This applies to the north as well as the south.

◀ Mr. MIDDLETON says : *Give everything room to grow. See how*

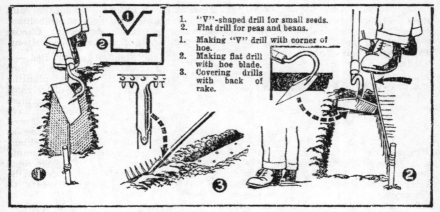

1. "V"-shaped drill for small seeds.
2. Flat drill for peas and beans.

1. Making "V" drill with corner of hoe.
2. Making flat drill with hoe blade.
3. Covering drills with back of rake.

The whole art of taking out drills

5. First Sowing of Celery.—The first sowing of celery can be made of a small variety, such as *Sutton's White Gem* or *Golden Self-blanching*. Sow in boxes in a greenhouse and keep in a temperature of 55° to 60° F. Leeks can also be sown in frames. Sow parsley inside for later pricking out in a frame. Parsley is slow in germinating out of doors, and it pays to have some plants on hand for putting out as soon as conditions are fit. It makes a pleasant path-edging and adds a finishing touch to the vegetable plot.

6. Maintain Succession of Seakale.—The last seakale to be forced inside should be lifted and brought in. The succession can be maintained from outside forcings. The central root or crown is used for forcing, the side or branching roots for propagating. Good thick pieces of these should be cut 6-in. long for "thongs," for propagation purposes. These should be tied in bundles and placed upright in boxes of soil under a greenhouse bench. They will produce buds and can be planted out later.

7. Paint Pruning Wounds.—In the fruit garden, first paint all large cuts made in pruning, using white lead paint, though Stockholm Tar is excellent. Such wounds are frequent where spur pruning or branch thinning has been practised. After the completion of all spraying and pruning, the ground, hardened by walking, should be forked and broken down.

8. Examine Blackcurrants.—Blackcurrants should be examined; those planted in autumn can be cut back rather more than half-way. If there are any swollen buds these should be picked off. They contain the big bud mite which can reduce considerably the fruitfulness of the bushes. Spraying to destroy this mite will be done later in the spring.

Wall fruit must be tied to their wires or nailed up. Do not use pieces of canvas or rag, because these make excellent breeding places for earwigs and other injurious pests.

9. Prepare Early Strawberries.—If you have plenty of frame room, you can produce a few early strawberries by growing some plants in pots. They should be potted from their small ones into 3½-in. pots and finally into 6-in. pots. Alternatively the frame can have a good depth of rich soil put in, and the young runners be planted in it

much you can get out of the garden, not how much you can get into it. ▶

during autumn. Lights are only put on in bad weather and in late winter to help flowering and fruiting. Plants in pots can be brought into a slightly warm greenhouse in succession for fruiting.

FEBRUARY—4th WEEK

1. Maintain Succession of Lettuces.— To maintain a succession of lettuce plants, put seedlings from earlier inside sowing into cold frames 8 to 12 in. apart. They can also be planted in a suitable position in the open garden and protected with cloches. Remember the ends of each row must be closed with glass or slate. If the weather is bad, see that all crops are adequately protected. Those in frames will need covering with mats when frost occurs. Cloches tend to get out of alignment and should be regularly adjusted. Crops in the open can be protected by covering with straw or bracken, or very twiggy branches from trees will help. Hurdles put on the windward side of any patch of vegetables help tremendously.

2. Break Down and Lime Soil.— When the soil is dry enough, and clear of frost, the job of breaking it down with a fork can begin. It is a good time to apply lime, thus doing two jobs at once. Break down all clods and lumps. This should be easy after hard weather, and produce a fine tilth and level surface to the plot. This forking is most important, particularly in producing a seed bed.

3. Maintain Succession of Seakale and Rhubarb.— The succession of seakale and forced rhubarb should be maintained from the outside bed. Force some heads by using boxes or barrels and covering with leaves or strawy manure. This need not be particularly hot. Cover rest of bed with straw.

4. Plant Onion Sets.— The following jobs can be done in the open garden according to climate and the part of the country in which you live. Plant onion sets. These are tiny onions used to produce crops where outside sowings

are normally a failure. Before the war they were imported from the Mediterranean area, where they were produced by sowing seeds on poor soil. The ideal size is about that of a large marble. Smaller than this they merely produce leaves, while larger ones run to seed. They should be planted in the same way as shallots, just pushing them into the soil without burying them. Distance apart, 12 in. by 6 in.

5. Sow Parsnips, Broad Beans, Carrots, etc.— Sow parsnips as soon as possible, also broad beans. This will probably be the first sowing of the latter in the north, but in the south will be successional. Sow shorthorn carrots, beetroot and radishes in warm spots under cloches. Plant autumn-sown onions.

6. Sow Early Peas, Sprouts and Summer Cabbage.— Sow early round-seeded peas of a dwarf variety. Round-seeded types are hardier and not so prone to decay as the wrinkled-seeded ones. Sow Brussels sprouts and summer cabbage in a cold frame. Make shallow drills 6 or 9 in. apart and sprinkle seed thinly along. Cover with a shallow layer of soil.

7. Pot Cucumbers and Tomatoes.— Cucumbers sown earlier should be potted into 5-in. . pots. Seedling tomatoes should be potted into 3½-in. pots. or if their planting out is to be delayed, into 5-in. pots. Prepare borders and receptacles in the greenhouse to receive them. On benches, troughs 12–15 in. wide and 10 in. deep should be made with planks, brick or turves, and filled with well-mixed soil, consisting of rough chopped loam, some decayed manure, sand, bone meal, and hydrated lime, or mortar rubble. Fill troughs at least a week before planting to allow soil to warm up. Put some broken brick at the bottom of troughs to act as drainage. Borders in the greenhouse should be well and deeply dug, dressing with lime, and digging in some straw. Before planting give a very thorough watering, so that subsoil is not dry, and allow a week or ten days for it to drain out.

◀ Mr. MIDDLETON says : *Potatoes are exotics. Do not paint*

MARCH—1st WEEK

1. Clear Land.—Land still occupied by crops should be gradually cleared as they are used. To accelerate the clearing, leeks and celery can be lifted and heeled in together, either in a frame or sheltered corner. This also checks the leeks and stops any tendency to run to seed. The celery should be deeply covered with soil to keep it crisp and white. Brussels sprouts, too, should be cleared as they are finished. The tops make useful greens even after all the buttons are used.

2. Beware of Cabbage Aphis !—Sprouts should not be allowed to remain right into spring, as it frequently happens that the dangerous pest, the *cabbage aphis*, overwinters on them in the egg stage. This aphis is one of the greenfly group of insects ; it is mealy and grey in colour, and, when it occurs in colonies, completely cripples the plants attacked. It has been on the increase of late years. From March onwards kales and sprouting broccoli will provide the mainstay of green foods. All rubbish should be added to the compost heap. Hard stalks of greens should be chopped up and put in the centre of the heap and given an ample dressing of rotting material.

3. Prepare Trenches for Peas and Beans.—It is a good idea to take out the trenches for tall peas and runner beans, to throw the soil at the side and leave for some weeks to weather. The trench should be 18-in. deep if manure is available to put in the bottom, 10–12 in. if none is obtainable.

4. Get Outside Seed Bed Ready.—As soon as possible prepare the outside seed bed. This can be in any suitable corner of the plot or garden. It need not be very big, as its chief use is to provide brassicas and leeks, and a lot of these can be produced in' a small space. Apply superphosphate of lime, three ounces to each square yard, and thoroughly fork in. Reduce the surface into as fine a condition as possible. Remove large stones. Rake down just before sowing time. Only do this forking when the soil is dry.

5. Prick Out Leeks, Onions, Celery.—Leeks and onions sown inside in heat will need pricking out into boxes. When established they should be moved into a cold frame for hardening off. Seedling celery from the February sowing should be pricked out when the third leaf shows.

6. Pot Tomatoes.—Pot tomatoes into 5-in. pots or plant into beds and borders where ready and warmed. As a substitute for troughs on benches, boxes may be used, while excellent crops are grown in cardboard containers. Special containers rather like small hat-boxes without lids or bottoms are obtainable. They should be placed on good, thick pieces of turf turned grass-down on the bench. Remember to give all plants a thorough soaking with water, and wherever they are grown, leave room for top dressing. If the white fly pest shows its presence, fumigate with the special White Fly Death (tetrachlorethane).

7. How to Use Cold Greenhouse.—A succession of food can be obtained

them until the sun has made its influence felt in the soil. ▶

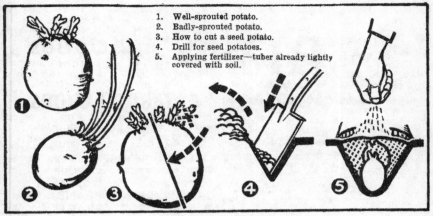

1. Well-sprouted potato.
2. Badly-sprouted potato.
3. How to cut a seed potato.
4. Drill for seed potatoes.
5. Applying fertilizer—tuber already lightly covered with soil.

Five pointers to good potato crops

from cold greenhouses by planting winter lettuce. When this is growing well, interplant with a cauliflower such as *Early London.* The lettuce will be cut in March or early April, the cauliflowers in May; and tomatoes can then be planted or even put in before the cauliflowers are cut.

8. Spray Strawberries, Support Raspberries, Prune Gooseberries.—Strawberries are sometimes attacked by a special mite (Tarsonemus), and it is necessary to spray with lime sulphur (1 part in 100) to control it. Go through the strawberry bed, and any new plants which have been lifted by frost should be firmed. Plants growing in pots can be fed with weak liquid manure. Raspberries should be supported by posts and horizontal wires, and the young canes which grew last year tied into position, shortening them a little at the same time. If you prune your gooseberry bushes do them now. They are usually spur-pruned.

MARCH—2nd WEEK

1. Fork Dry Soil.—Press on with forking soil when it is dry enough. This presents little difficulty on light, well-drained soils, but on heavier ones opportunities are restricted. In the western side of the country it is often difficult owing to rain. Much harm can be done by working on heavy land when it is wet. This forking may not be possible until April.

2. Get Ahead with Parsnips.—Many sowings should be made out of doors as the soil is brought into a fine condition. Parsnips need a long season to become fully developed and, if not already sown, this should be done without delay. Sow in drills 15 or 18 in. apart, and put a pinch of seeds at intervals of 9 in. rather than sprinkle some all along the drill. As parsnips are slow in germinating, it is good to make a thin sowing of radish or lettuce in the drill. These mark its position and permit hoeing to be done before the parsnips appear. They will also mature and can be used.

3. Sow Onions Outdoors.—Onions, too, must be sown out of doors immediately. The bed should be well prepared, and drills drawn at 12 in. apart. Sow the seed thinly; experience shows that a bigger weight per row is obtained if the seedlings are left unthinned. Some growers leave them until fairly large, then draw out the surplus plants and use them as salad onions, leaving

◀**Mr. MIDDLETON** says : *Soil is the basis of life. Take care of it.*▶

one plant at every 6 in. It frequently happens that, leaving them until large enough for salad use and then pulling them spoils those left in. Onions for salad purposes should be grown separately, and a row can be sown now. *White Lisbon* is a good variety, and for pickles *Silverskin Pickling* is also useful.

4. Sow Spinach Outside.—Spinach can be sown on a warm border outside, or elsewhere under cloches. Leeks can be sown on the main seed bed, as well as cabbage, cauliflowers, and Brussels sprouts. Another sowing of peas can be made in southern areas. In the north, sow broad beans.

5. In and Out of the Greenhouse.—In the greenhouse make another sowing of tomatoes if a succession of plants is required. Celeriac seeds can now be sown in boxes. Brassicas raised in the greenhouse should be pricked out into a cold frame. Lettuce raised inside can be planted in the open garden or under cloches. Cauliflowers similarly raised or wintered in a frame can be planted out. Sage and thyme can be sown in boxes to raise plants for putting out later.

6. Harden Off Onions and Leeks.—Plants such as onions and leeks, which have been pricked off into boxes, should be moved into a cold frame gradually to harden off. They will want care and little ventilation at first, but later should be given plenty of air until the lights can be left off altogether.

7. Plant Out Early Potatoes.—First early potatoes can be planted in warm gardens. Give them 15–18 in. between the rows, and 12 in. between the tubers. Take out a drill 5 to 6 in. deep and cover in the tubers. The soil should be flat and not ridged at first. Draw up ridges only as the potatoes grow. If frost threatens after the tops are through, cover with soil, or use bracken or twigs. In the north a few tubers could be planted in a frame to give very early new potatoes.

8. Feed and Support Fruit Trees.—As March is often a windy month, it will pay to examine the stakes and ties of fruit trees to see that they are secure. Proceed with applying fertilizer to the trees. Fruit trees often suffer from deficiencies of certain food elements, potash being one of the most common. Nitrogen is also frequently needed, but there is usually enough phosphorus. A good general fertilizer can be given, or make up a dressing by mixing 3 parts sulphate of ammonia with 2 parts sulphate of potash, if obtainable, and apply at the rate of 6 ounces per square yard. The fertilizer is usually given all around the trees as far out as the branches spread. Lightly fork it in and tidy up beneath the trees.

9. Complete Planting of Fruit Trees.—March generally gives the last opportunity for planting before growth begins. It should be completed without delay. Old trees are sometimes regrafted with better varieties. An older method is top-grafting, whereby the main branches, except one, are cut back to near their base and grafts of a suitable variety inserted in the stumps. The one main branch is left to take the rush of sap from the roots. It is done when the others are established. A newer method is to cut off all spurs and side-branches, leaving only the main framework. Grafts are inserted all along the branches. There are various methods of inserting them. This method is known as "frame-working."

MARCH—3rd WEEK

1. Work on Sandy Soil.—Light sandy soils can now be dug. These dry soils, consisting of particles which so easily pack together, bed down again after digging, and if done in early winter soon look as though they have never been touched. They might just as well be done in spring. Another reason is that such soils are expensive of manure. Sandy soils permit free percolation of air between the particles, and as plenty of air stimulates the decay of manure by encouraging the bacteria which bring about this decay, manure tends to disappear. If it is dug in during early

◀ **Mr. MIDDLETON says :** *A cabbage which is not transplanted* winter, therefore, it will decay and the foods in it will be released, washed from the soil, and lost to the plants. Heavier soils are colder and do not permit air to move so freely. In addition, a tilth is easily produced on light soils, while heavy soils require a lot of weathering. Manure can therefore be incorporated in winter, and very little of value be lost. Light soils have many advantages, in that they drain quickly after rain and can be worked on without doing damage. They quickly warm up in spring and are thus ideal for early seed sowings. Their disadvantages are a tendency to suffer from drought in summer, and to be weedy. They require much manure or humus-making material added. They are often deficient in lime.

2. Plant Early Potatoes.—Begin planting early potatoes wherever possible. In the south and parts of the midlands doubtless some can be got in now. They should be well sprouted and have the number of sprouts reduced to two, unless you prefer a larger number of small potatoes. Unhealthy tubers should be destroyed. Do not plant any suffering from dry rot, as they merely decay in the soil. By planting now, new potatoes can be obtained really early.

3. Plant Out Cauliflowers, Onions, Cabbage.—Cauliflowers can be planted out, too, and so can the autumn-sown onions. Some early cabbage, such as *Velocity*, can also be sown to provide a supply after the spring cabbage are finished. The main supply of greens comes from kales and sprouting broccoli. If the spring cabbages were planted close together, as is sometimes done, they will now be getting crowded, and alternate plants should be pulled out and used as spring greens, leaving the others to heart up into proper cabbages.

4. Attend to Asparagus Beds.—Asparagus beds should now receive attention. Manure will have been spread on top in early winter. This should be forked in carefully. Soil will have been washed down into the alleyways on

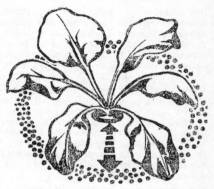

Always apply your fertilizer in a circle a short distance from stem of the plant

each side of the bed. This should be put on the beds again, the sides be made square and neat, and the paths cleaned. A post at each corner of the bed is useful. A dressing of salt is often given; it helps to keep down weeds, but is not necessary for the asparagus itself.

5. Outdoor Tomatoes.—Plants of tomatoes for growing out of doors can be raised from seed sown now. Most of the ordinary standard varieties seem to be quite successful in the open (i.e., *Best of All, Market King, Potentate*), and to do better than the special outdoor ones. In northern areas where tomatoes can normally be grown outside, *Early Sunrise* is good, as it ripens quickly, but it is a light cropper. Tomatoes planted in beds require care with watering. The normal practice is to soak the plants before putting in and not to water again until the first truss of flowers is set. More trouble is caused to tomatoes by injudicious watering than by anything else, particularly in unheated houses. Plants growing on benches, being better drained and probably with hot-water pipes below, may need watering sooner than those in beds. Those planted earlier, and growing away, will need the help of a rabbit's

will heart up much earlier than one that is. Try it both ways. ▶

tail to set their fruit. The first truss is always difficult to set, and the plants should be helped as much as possible. A moist atmosphere helps setting. Plants growing in large pots should be limited to three trusses per plant.

6. Spawn Mushroom Beds.—Mushroom beds made earlier should now be cooling a little if they have been properly built. Fermentation will have reached its height and will be falling back. When the temperature is about 75° F., the spawn should be pushed into the manure. Pieces about the size of a walnut should be used.

7. Look Out for Fruit Diseases.— Blackcurrants will soon be growing. Where big bud mite is present it is usual to spray with lime sulphur solution when the leaves are about the size of a shilling, which may be any time between now and mid-April. It is now that the mites begin to move and are most vulnerable. The solution should be 1 gallon to 13 gallons of water. It is wise at this time also to purchase any spraying materials likely to be needed in summer, such as nicotine. When spraying blackcurrants, strawberries can also be sprayed for Tarsonemus mite, but a weaker solution must be used—1 part in 100.

Grease bands should not be removed from the trunks of fruit trees where they have been used to catch the wingless females of various moths which attempt to climb the trees. As there is danger from March moth, leave the bands on for a week or two yet.

MARCH—4th WEEK

1. Last Chances for Good Digging.— Those who did not succeed in digging most of the garden before Christmas, and have since been held up by bad weather, should press on without delay. Land dug early breaks down easily when forked and produces a good sowing tilth. It is much more difficult to do this on land only just turned over.

2. More Early Potatoes Now.—It may be possible to begin planting early potatoes even in the north, and no opportunity should be wasted in getting them in. Later frosts will not trouble them much. Some gardeners who have heavy land prefer to leave the digging of the potato patch until now and to plant as they dig. There is something to be said for it, but only under special circumstances.

3. Plant Shallots and Garlic.—Do not delay any longer your planting of shallots. Garlic may be planted now, using the same method of cultivation as for shallots, except that each garlic bulb is broken up into separate small cloves and these planted separately. Horseradish must be put in now also. Pieces of root 3-in. long, called " thongs," are pushed into the soil in an upright position, the top being just covered. Choose an out-of-the-way corner for this plant.

4. Make Asparagus Bed.—If you have room for an asparagus bed, make and plant it now. In preparing the site, remember that this is a permanent crop and may remain in the same place for twenty or more years. The ground, which must be well drained, should therefore be double dug and have plenty of manure worked in, as well as a goodly amount of bone meal. The bed should be 4½–5-ft. wide, which will take three rows at 18 in. apart. Three ridges of soil a few inches high should be put down to mark the rows. Buy good 3-year-old crowns, all male, if possible. The sexes are borne on different plants, and the male is preferred as energy is not wasted in producing seed nor are seedlings spread over the bed later. The crowns should be placed on the ridges 15 in. apart, the roots being spread to the sides. Cover with 6 in. of soil. A 2-ft. path can be taken out all round, and the soil placed on the bed.

5. Sow Parsley, Thyme, Sage, Celery.—Parsley can be sown outside, and so can thyme and sage. They can be sown in good patches, as drifts or as edgings to paths. The main supply of

◀ **Mr. MIDDLETON** says : *If you are not successful with onions, grow*

celery should be sown inside now. Celeriac, too, can be sown.

6. Stake Cucumbers.—Cucumbers raised earlier and potted into 5-in. pots will probably be 18 in. or so long and ready to tie to a small stake. They should be planted in a warm house where a good temperature can be maintained. A rich mixture of soil should be made up for them, adding plenty of well-rotted manure and some good fertilizer. In ordinary greenhouses they are best grown on benches, but in special cucumber houses, the roofs of which slope right down to the soil, they are grown on the floor. On the bench a 3-in. layer of rough leaves should be put, and on this a 6–9-in. layer of soil. Mounds of soil are made on this 9 in. deep and 1½ to 2 ft. apart. Some growers omit the deep layer of soil and just make mounds on the leaves, adding to them as the cucumbers grow. Plant the cucumbers carefully, no deeper than they are in the pots. The top of the mound should be rounded, not hollowed, so that water will not hang around the stem and cause canker.

7. Attack Apple Pests.—As the leaves of apples burst they should be sprayed with nicotine, to control the apple sucker. This is a bad pest; it stunts and deforms young leaves, attacks buds and blossoms, and considerably reduces the crop. Tar-distillate washes in winter are the usual control, because they kill the eggs, but where persistent trouble is experienced, additional nicotine spray destroys the young larvæ. Greasebands should be freshened up with grease to catch the female March moth as it ascends the trees: also erect bird-scarers.

MARCH—5th WEEK

1. Maintain Succession of Potatoes.—Continue planting potatoes as conditions permit. As soon as the earlies are finished, carry on with second earlies. In the south those planted earlier may be through the soil and will need protection in case of frost. Earth up and place twigs over the rows.

2. Sow Lettuce and Sweet Corn.—Cos lettuce can be sown inside in boxes or in a frame, for later planting out. Sweet corn seeds can also be sown inside now, as well as out of doors later on. Space the seeds out at 2–3-in. intervals in boxes of good soil, or sow broadcast and pot up later.

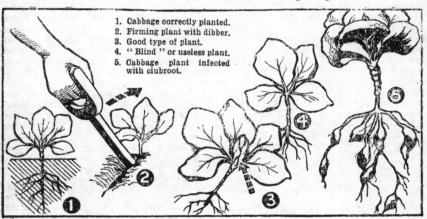

1. Cabbage correctly planted.
2. Firming plant with dibber.
3. Good type of plant.
4. " Blind " or useless plant.
5. Cabbage plant infected with clubroot.

Five important facts about cabbages

shallots. They are an excellent substitute, and much easier to grow. ▶

3. Case Mushroom Beds.—Mushroom beds which were spawned a week or fortnight ago should now be ready for "casing." Before this is done make sure the spawn is running. Examine the places where the spawn pieces were pushed in, and if grey threads are radiating out from them they are right. To case, cover the bed with a 2-in. layer of poor soil or subsoil free from weed seeds. Specially mixed soil is not necessary.

4. Deal with Clubroot Disease.—If you have trouble with clubroot disease of brassica crops, take precautions when planting out your crops. Young brassica seedling plants, in boxes or frames, should be twice watered with a solution of corrosive sublimate (mercuric bichloride) which is a scheduled poison, at a strength of 1 ounce in $12\frac{1}{2}$ gallons of water (1 in 2,000). When planting, take out the holes first, pour $\frac{1}{2}$-pint of the solution in, then put in the plant and water it with the solution three weeks later. This treatment also helps against attacks of cabbage root fly, and should be used on soils badly infected with clubroot. On soils where it is only suspected, the land should be limed; and as plants are put out, the holes should be dusted with a mixture of hydrated lime and flowers of sulphur.

5. Train Cucumbers.—Cucumbers should be trained up wires in the greenhouse. The stake to which they are originally tied should be fastened to the bottom wire. A cane can be fastened to the wires up which the main stem can be trained. This stem should be allowed to grow up to the top of the house and then stopped by pinching out the growing point. Side shoots are allowed to develop from the axil of each leaf on the main stem, but are stopped at every second leaf. One cucumber is taken from each joint on the side shoot. The stopping of these at each second leaf as they develop encourages rapid development of the fruits and evens out the crop.

6. Sow Root Crops Outside.—Shorthorn or intermediate carrots can now be sown outside in suitable circumstances, and so can globe beetroot. It is a little early for the long beet. Six-week turnips can also be sown.

7. Look to Fruit, and Pests.—Fruit in greenhouses needs careful management as to ventilation, temperature, and humidity of the atmosphere. The fruit trees themselves should be syringed daily to encourage healthy growth and to discourage red spider mite.

Any signs of aphis attacks on outside fruit should be dealt with immediately, as so many of these creatures cause leaf curl, and once inside the folds of twisted leaves they are immune from attack. The winter wash should have prevented an attack, but if this was omitted, use a nicotine wash and apply it so as to hit the insects.

It frequently seems that most of the operations in the fruit garden are against pests and diseases. Control of these is essential to the production of healthy fruit, and there are many of them.

8. Spray Apples and Pears.—Apples and pears should be sprayed now with lime-sulphur to control scab. This first spray is in the " green bud " stage and a strength of 1 in 40 is used. The lime-sulphur is bought as a proprietary article and should be mixed according to the makers' instructions. Lead arsenate (poison) can be mixed with this spray to control caterpillars. Some varieties of apple are said to be " sulphur shy," e.g., *Stirling Castle*, *Beauty of Bath*, *Lane's Prince Albert* and *Newton Wonder*. For these, Bordeaux mixture should be used instead.

◄ Mr. MIDDLETON says : *Do not sow runner*

APRIL—1st WEEK

1. Support Peas.—Peas from earlier sowings will need staking. Dwarf varieties of only $1\frac{1}{2}$ to $2\frac{1}{2}$ ft. will do well without any support, but even with these it is better to arrange a little, particularly with the first sowings. Twigs provide the best support and should be inserted as soon as the seedlings show. For peas that are planted out, supports are put in immediately. Push them in firmly, and keep them vertical or leaning slightly inwards. Allow at least 6 in. over the advertised height of the variety. Trim the twigs lightly with hedge shears to give a neat appearance.

2. Counter Enemies of Peas.—Early-sown peas are subject to a number of troubles. In wet weather they germinate, but instead of growing they decay, consequently only half or even less will grow. This frequently happens in the colder and wetter parts of the country when sowings are made somewhat too early. It pays, no matter where you are, to sow the seeds a little thicker than is usual in the summer. Mice are a nuisance in the early stages, as they scratch up and eat the peas. Birds, too, will also scratch them out. To prevent this, roll or shake the seeds in red lead which has been first moistened with paraffin. Too much paraffin will prevent germination. When the seedlings are through, birds—sparrows in particular—pull them to pieces. There are numerous ways of preventing this, and perhaps the easiest is to push short sticks in along each side of the row, and criss-cross black cotton over the seedlings. The birds, upon contact

with the cotton, which they do not see, are startled. Other things which can be used are wire netting covers (special ones can be bought), or string tied along the row; or horticultural pepper dust can be dusted over the leaves, or quassia sprayed on them to make them bitter. The twigs when put in give no protection from birds unless black cotton is entwined over the seedlings.

3. Don't be Too Early with Tomatoes !—Tomatoes planted in heated houses now will provide a late summer crop. This is the earliest time that unheated houses should be used. There is little gained by planting earlier, and even now it is better to delay if the weather is hard. The soil is normally so cold that root growth is slow. The commonest causes of failure in unheated houses are badly prepared soil and incorrect watering. By giving too much water in the early stages the soil is kept cold and the plants will not grow.

4. Start New Compost Heap.—The compost heap, to which you have been adding all the winter, should be completed now so that it will be thoroughly decayed by the autumn and can be used to dig in. A new heap should be started to take the summer rubbish.

5. Plant Out Onions.—Onions raised inside should now be planted out if conditions permit. Great care is necessary with this work. It is important that the plants are not put in too deeply or they will grow thick-necked, while if they are put in too shallow they will be twisted and turned by the wind and fail to get hold. They should be planted as shallow as possible, while

beans out of doors until the lilac is in bloom. ▶

still making them firm. The normal depth is about that of the small bulb which will be swelling at the base. On light soils they can be deeper, as the bulb, when it really begins to swell, can push the soil to one side. On heavier soils there is more difficulty. If planted too deep, the bulb, when it wants to swell, cannot shoulder the soil away. Thus it is forced upwards and the plant becomes thick-necked. In exposed gardens give some cloche protection for a short time, until they have got hold.

6. Sow Long-Rooted Carrots.—Long-rooted carrots, such as *St. Valery*, can now be sown. They need a long season to get the best from them. Trenches prepared for tall peas can now be filled in. A layer of manure should be put in the bottom and some of it be mixed with the soil as it is returned. Bone meal should be dusted in with it. Allow a day or two to settle and then sow the seeds. The trench should be 12-in. wide. When it is filled in, a drill should be left for the seeds. Cover with soil, but leave a slight depression, which will prove useful for watering later on.

7. Plant Seakale Thongs.—Seakale thongs, which were taken earlier and put in soil under a greenhouse bench or similar place, will have produced buds, and can now be planted. For lifting and forcing inside they should be planted singly, 18 in. apart, in rows 2 ft. apart. For forcing in the open, plant in triangles with a foot between each thong and 3 ft. from triangle to triangle.

APRIL—2nd WEEK

1. Finish Onion Planting.—Finish planting onions as soon as possible. Do not risk failure by putting them out when the land is sticky. Onions thrive best on a bed which is rich and firm, and do not like a loose, newly-dug soil. Therefore this portion of the garden should be dug well before Christmas so that it will have time to settle.

In spring, dress with the necessary fertilizers, lightly fork, tread and rake down. Where soil is heavy and the climate wet, however, treading the soil produces only a sodden, sticky result. If wet weather prevents soil from drying out, boards must be put down to take your weight. This is often necessary when *sowing* onions. In the north main-crop onions should now be sown without delay. Sow onions for salad purposes if not already done.

2. Sow Spinach and Peas.—Spinach can be sown outside. A good variety for now is the *Long-Standing Round*, which does not run to seed so readily as the ordinary round type.

A successional sowing of peas should be made. Sow at intervals of a fortnight to keep up a supply right through the summer. In the south, the varieties of medium height can now be put in; but in the north the dwarf varieties will be better at present. Stick to dwarf forms right through if you cannot get staking material. Wire pea supports are the best, then twigs. But do not use string or anything like that. Large mesh string nets are good if they are strong, but some of those sold are too weak.

3. Sow Radish and Lettuce Outdoors.—Sow radish out of doors, choosing a position between rows of cabbage or cauliflowers, or between peas and beans. This quick-growing crop can be grown and matured before the other vegetables are fully grown, so this is a good way to use the wide pieces of land between the rows. The method is known as intercropping, and is a way to get more than one crop from a piece of land. Lettuce can be used, too, and plants may be put out now. A single row between two rows of cabbage is enough; more is generally wasteful. Spinach is also suitable for intercropping, as it grows quickly.

4. Fertilize Potatoes, and Plant More.—Draw a little soil up to the potatoes planted during last month, which are showing. Apply a dressing of a potato fertilizer between the rows and mix it with the soil when drawing it up. Plant more potatoes.

◀ Mr. MIDDLETON says : *Pruning blackcurrants, raspberries,*

5. Sow Salsify, Chicory, Runner Beans.—Salsify can be sown now. Sprinkle the seed thinly in drills a foot apart. Chicory can be sown for forcing in winter. Sow in drills 12 in. apart and thin seedlings to 9 in. Runner beans, which will not stand frost, may be sown in boxes and brought on in a cold frame to be planted when danger of frost is past. Dwarf beans can be treated the same.

6. Plant Out Cabbage and Sprouts.—Plant out cabbages and Brussels sprouts. The sooner the sprouts are out and growing the better.

7. Sow Carrots and Turnips.—Sow long-rooted carrots. On heavy land it is good to bore holes 18 in. to 2 ft. deep and 2-3 in. across. Use a crowbar or strong pole and fill up holes with a mixed light soil such as is used in the greenhouse. Allow 9×15 in. for these large varieties. Sprinkle a few seeds at the top of each hole and cover with soil. Later, thin to one good seedling. Suitable varieties are *St. Valery* (which is an excellent show carrot, being smooth), *Altrincham* and *Long Red Surrey*. Sow six-week turnips.

8. Spray Fruit Bushes and Trees.—Spray blackcurrants for mite and gooseberries for American gooseberry mildew. This mildew is a bad disease. If you get it you must take steps to prevent its recurrence. Spray with lime-sulphur 1 in 60 (some varieties will

stand a slightly stronger solution) immediately after the fruit has set. Some varieties will not stand lime-sulphur, and ammonium polysulphide should then be used. It can be bought as a proprietary article. The yellow varieties are the most sensitive ; washing soda is sometimes employed on them. Spray cherries for aphis.

9. Look to Frames.—Harden off brassicas, etc., in frames. All lights should be off now.

APRIL—3rd WEEK

This is a very active period in the garden. Many sowings are made outside of the hardier things, while the less hardy are raised inside and hardened off for planting when frost is past.

1. Pot Sweet Corn.—Do not let sweet corn, sown in small pots, get root bound, but transfer to 5-in. pots. Those raised in boxes can also be potted up. A greatly increased interest has been shown in this delicacy since our American allies came over. Unfortunately its successful culture is limited to the south and midlands, though it has been grown quite well in protected gardens further north. In most parts of the

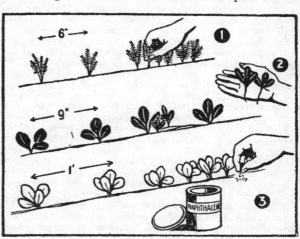

THINNING CROPS AND FUMIGATING SOIL

In thinning plants see that good ones remain. If weather is dry, moisten ground with naphthalene and water.

and other plants consists of removing old to make room for new. ▶

country it is necessary to raise plants in greenhouses for planting out later, though in mild districts seeds can be sown direct in the garden in May. In others, success has been obtained by sowing under cloches.

2. Prepare Tomatoes for Outdoors.— Tomatoes being raised for outdoor growing should be pricked out or potted on if ready. Try to time them so as to be a foot high and ready for planting out at the end of May or early in June. If there is room to put them into 5-in. pots they have better chances of success, and they should have one truss of flowers showing at the time of planting. Tomatoes now growing under glass need plenty of attention. Water only when the first truss is set. Do not soak all the border, but apply the water just round the roots. Adequate stakes or ties must be provided for each plant. Those on benches can be fastened to wires near the roof of the house, while those on the floor of the greenhouse must be trained up strings. As they go, remove all side shoots, which arise in the axils of the leaves. Use a rabbit's tail to fertilize the flowers, particularly early in the year. Damping down the walks maintains the humid atmosphere which is necessary to get complete bunches of fruits. Trusses which develop only a few full-sized fruits and a lot of small ones suffer from "dry set," which means that some flowers have not been pollenated. Later in the year ample ventilation and sunlight help proper setting. Careful ventilation is essential, the main aim being to maintain a steady temperature of about 60° F. Air must therefore be put on the houses when the sun raises the temperature, and taken off a little before the sun goes down.

Sow vegetable marrows now in the greenhouse. Push the seeds singly into small pots. They must not be planted out of doors till May, when the danger of sharp frost is over.

3. Make Up Celery Trenches.—Celery trenches should be made up now to allow time for settling down before

planting. A thick layer of manure should be placed in the bottom and soil placed over it. The trench should be 10-in. deep, and the surplus soil rounded off at the sides to provide a growing place for lettuce, or beans, etc., and for blanching the celery later. The trenches should be 12–15-in. wide for a single row, but at least 18-in. for a double row.

Most of the winter greens should be sown now, such as pre-Christmas broccoli, kales, etc.

4. Spray Apples and Pears.—Apples and pears should be given their second anti-scab spray. It is usually applied in what is known as the pink-bud stage, i.e., when the buds are just showing pink. Use lime-sulphur at a strength of 1 in 60, apart from the sulphur-shy varieties, such as Cox's Orange Pippin, on which Bordeaux mixture must be used.

5. Planting Work.—Plant out broad beans if they have been delayed. Plant out cauliflowers for succession, and make successional sowings of turnips and beet. Continue potato planting. Turn over the land as greens are used. Hoe between outside crops.

APRIL—4th WEEK

1. Sow Calabresse, Pickling Onions and Garlic.—Calabresse can now be sown in the outside seed bed. This is a form of cauliflower which provides a green head in summer and, when this is cut, produces shoots for winter use. Pickling onions can be sown. *Queen Pickling* or *Silverskin Pickling* are good varieties. Put the seeds in thinly on the onion bed. Shallots should be growing now and will benefit from a dressing of general fertilizer hoed in between the rows. Onions planted out in March and now established can also have a light fertilizer dressing. Garlic may be planted in exactly the same way as shallots, except that the old bulbs are first broken up and the small sections planted separately.

2. Look to Your Frames.—Ridge cucumbers can be sown for planting

◀ **Mr. MIDDLETON** says : *All pruning should have a purpose.*

outside or growing in a frame. Ordinary cucumbers are also grown easily in frames, and seeds should be sown now. Self-blanching celery is ideal for growing in cold frames after other seedlings have been used up. Seeds sown in boxes inside will come in for this purpose.

3. Plant First Leeks.—The first leeks should be planted now for those who are exhibiting or who like to have them early. Exhibitors must prepare their soil especially well, using manure and fertilizer. Leeks do like a rich soil. There are two ways of growing them—in trenches and in holes. The trench method is best for the exhibitor. It is made in the same way as a celery trench and is about 6-in. deep. The plants are put in 2- or 3-in. deep in single or double rows. As the plants grow they are earthed up with soil to produce well-blanched stems.

4. Cutting Asparagus.—Asparagus is now ready for cutting and must be done carefully. Special knives can be obtained for the work, but a good, long, narrow-bladed knife will serve. Cut the stalks when 4 or 5 in. long and insert the knife beneath the soil.

5. Sow Maincrop Beet.—Maincrop beet should be sown now, especially in the north. The long-rooted varieties in particular need a long season to develop. The globe forms will mature more quickly. Earlier sowings should be thinned out before they get over-crowded. In making sowings it is much better to sow continuously along the drill rather than in pinches at intervals, as with parsnips. If there is any failure of the seed, sowing in pinches often lets you down, whereas a continuous sowing usually provides enough to complete a row. Beet are better not transplanted, but blanks can be filled by carefully moving seedlings from one part of the row to another. Salsify sown earlier can be thinned to 6 in. apart.

6. Earth-up Potatoes ; Prepare Marrow Beds.—Potatoes growing should be kept earthed-up as they grow. Sites for vegetable marrows can be prepared.

They can be grown on heaps of soil and soil-covered shelters, but holes must be dug out 12 in. deep and 18 in. square, manure put in and some good soil to fill up. The trailing varieties are ideal for such positions.

7. Bark Ring Fruit Trees.—The bark ringing of over-vigorous fruit trees can be done any time from now till early June. A ring of bark $\frac{1}{8}$-in. thick is taken out all round the trunk of the tree, or alternatively two half-rings, one above the other with about 4 in. between them and on opposite sides of the stem, are cut out. The purpose is to check the flow of elaborated food from the leaves down to the roots and to keep more of it in the branches. General growth is thus checked, as the surplus food in the branches has a tendency to congregate in the stronger buds and turn them into fruit spurs instead of shoots. The cuts should be covered with adhesive tape or painted.

8. Hunt Gooseberry Pests.—A common pest of gooseberries is the caterpillar of the magpie moth. Its presence is not always noticed until it has cleared much of the foliage. Examine the centre of bushes for attacked leaves, and if signs of the pest are there, spray with derris. Left unchecked they will destroy every leaf on the shrubs.

9. Sow, Plant and Hoe.—Make any necessary successional sowings. Prick out celeriac sown earlier. Dress shallots with fertilizer. Prepare outdoor tomato sites. Plant out parsley. Thin out salsify to 6 in. Hoe around fruit trees and bushes.

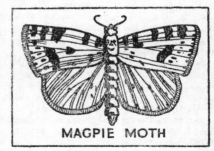

MAGPIE MOTH

If you don't know why you are cutting a shoot, don't cut it. ▶

MAY—1st WEEK

1. Look to Spring and Winter Greens.
—Some of the late winter and spring
greens will now be coming to an end.
As they do so they should be lifted and
the land prepared for re-cropping.
Spring cabbage, if it matures at its
correct time, should be now well in use.
It sometimes happens in some parts of
the country that it only begins to heart
up now in May and continues in use
until the end of June.

It is tempting to leave the stalks in
the ground, for they will certainly break
and produce further greens and even
further hearts. Sometimes two or three
small heads are produced from each
stalk.

This, however, upsets the cropping
plan, and, anyway, when these greens
come in they clash with autumn cabbage,
which are superior. So clear the stalks
as soon as the heads are cut. Even in
the north, where most seed sowings
must be completed by the end of June,
there are many crops which can be put
in immediately after the cabbage. It
is a good tip, if manure is hard to get,
to sow a crop such as mustard for digging in later. This is known as green
manuring and is a useful way of enriching the soil.

2. Sow Runner Beans Outside.—
In the south and midlands runner beans
and dwarf French beans may now be
risked outside. By the time they are
through the danger of severe frost will
be fairly remote. It is still early to
plant out those raised under glass, but
they should be hardened off as
much as possible.

**3. Sow Late Greens ; Look Out for
Club Root.**—Late greens such as broccoli, savoys, *January King* cabbage,
can now be sown on the outside seed
bed. Water with corrosive sublimate,
one ounce in twelve gallons of water,
if previous crops have been infected
with club root. Brassicas which are
planted out should be protected against
cabbage root fly so far as is possible.
This pest has been particularly troublesome of late years. Its special partiality
is cauliflower, but it attacks every member of the cabbage family. If you are
using corrosive sublimate for club root,
then this will almost certainly control it.
With plants that are already affected it
is the only check on spreading of the
trouble. For instance, if a few plants
flag, and on pulling them up you find
small white grubs feeding on the stems,
do not hesitate, but get some sublimate
and water them with it. *Remember
that this is a dangerous poison and needs
careful handling.* It is claimed
for calomel dust that it offers good
means of control, but it is not 100 per
cent. effective. Naphthalene hoed into
the soil around the plants is a deterrent.

4. Sow Beet and Sweet Corn.—Sow
seakale beet and spinach beet in rows
18-in. apart. Put the seed in pinches
at intervals of 9 in. Sweet corn seeds
may be sown out of doors now in the
south, but they may need cloche
protection for a short time.

5. Beware Woolly Aphis.—Woolly
aphis is a serious pest of apples and
every effort should be made to check its
development, particularly on young
trees. It is a small sucking insect which

◀ Mr. MIDDLETON says : *Little and often is the golden rule*

lives in colonies in cracks in the bark, which it extends, and surrounds itself with a mass of wool-like threads. This wool makes it difficult to control. Winter spraying with tar distillate helps to reduce it, but it always seems to reappear. When the wool tufts are seen they should be brushed off with a stiff brush dipped in methylated spirit.

6. Keep Strawberries Clean.—When the flower stalks of strawberries appear, clean straw should be placed around the plants to keep the fruit clean. It must be put down carefully and the trusses placed over it. Special mats of straw can be purchased for the purpose.

7. Sow and Plant.—Sow and plant out lettuce. Sow more peas, and plant out tall peas raised inside. Finish planting potatoes. Thin parsnips and other seedlings. Prick out celery and celeriac. Sow scorzonera out of doors, and radishes for succession. Hoe and keep down weeds.

MAY—2nd WEEK

1. Plant Out Celery and Celeriac.—Plant out celery and celeriac. Celery is normally planted in trenches in single or double rows. The single row is easier to manage when earthing up. The plants should be strong and healthy, and when lifted from the boxes should have a good ball of roots. Set the plants out 9 in. apart. Keep a watch for slug attacks. Water with liquid manure : celery being a bog plant requires an abundance of water. Dust with old soot often, to keep the celery fly away. Celeriac, which is grown for its turnip-like root, requires a rich soil and much feeding to get really good roots. Normally it is grown on the flat, not in trenches. Plant 12 in. by 18 in. Treat as celery for pest control, and feed it at the same time. It is a fine vegetable for soup, and is excellent boiled.

2. Thin Out Seedlings.—Many rows of seedlings will need thinning out from time to time. This can be done at one stage, though normal practice is to do it twice. The first time the rows are reduced and specimens left about twice as thick as is necessary. This leaves plenty to cover failures. The alternate plants are removed at the final thinning. With carrots the disturbance of the row loosens the soil and permits the carrot fly to lay its eggs near the roots of the plants, and the pungent smell attracts the pest. Immediately after thinning, the rows should be watered and naphthalene hoed in along each side of the rows. Where the fly has proved a nuisance in the past it is better to sow the seeds sparingly and to leave the rows unthinned. This suggestion applies only to stump-rooted and intermediate varieties. Long-rooted varieties must, of course, be thinned.

3. Onions and Their Enemies.—The same sort of thing applies to onions which, when sown out of doors and thinned, attract the onion fly where fly is prevalent. It is better to leave them unthinned and take a crop of smaller onions. Anyway, the total weight of such a crop is usually greater than with a thinned crop, and they keep better. Calomel dust is the normal specific for controlling the fly, and it should be dusted along the rows. Failing calomel use naphthalene, or paraffin and sand, mixed together in a bucket and dusted alongside the rows. The paraffin smell discourages the fly. Some growers favour a row or two of parsley amongst the onions, as the smell of parsley is said to discourage the fly. *Once onion fly is experienced the site of the crop must be changed the next year, even though they have been grown for years in that one spot.* Early digging after clearing the crop exposes many of the pests to frost and the birds.

4. Plant Cucumbers.—Cucumbers can now be planted in frames. If it is a cold frame it is a good idea to make up a hot-bed with manure, to cover it with soil, and when it is cooling down, to plant the cucumbers. They will do well in frames, though the fruit may not be so straight as the greenhouse ones. Their training is identical to those inside.

with fertilizers : a little less rather than a little more. ▶

5. Sow Swedes and Turnips.—Swede turnips should be sown now in the north if they are to achieve full development. The round turnips such as *Golden Ball* should also be sown now. Put the swedes in drills 18-in. apart, and the turnips 12-in. apart.

6. Sow and Plant.—Sow maincrop beet and haricot beans. Plant out late cauliflowers and New Zealand spinach. Apply mulches to any fruit trees that need it. Protect beans outside if weather is unseasonable.

MAY—3rd WEEK

1. Thinning and Planting.—There will be much thinning out of seedlings in May from sowings made in April. This operation is most important and should be done before the young plants get too crowded with their roots tangled together, and by their competition with each other weaken those which are left.

Plant out crops from the seed bed and frames as necessary. If frost for the year seems to be over, some of the more tender crops, such as runner beans raised in frames, can be set out.

2. How is Your Plan Working?—The garden should now be getting nice and full, but there should still be room for a few later crops. To speak of the necessity for planting and sowing at different times is to emphasise the need for a plan. When no plan is being used it is fatally easy to put in a few extra rows of cabbage, cauliflowers, turnips, or whatever it is, and to leave no room for other essential crops.

3. Plant Out Lettuce.—Cos lettuce raised under glass may now be planted out. Allow 12 in. from plant to plant. A good place for them is on the ridge of soil at each side of the celery trench. A few seeds can be sown out of doors also to provide a succession to the others. Planting of cabbage lettuce can be done now. Later plantings are not so successful, as the young plants have difficulty in becoming established in summer. It is better to sow thinly in drills and to thin the seedlings out

when an inch or two high. Never allow lettuce seedlings to become crowded, as they grow soft and decay early. Some people like to use the thinnings as salads, but in so doing they rarely thin out the rows in good time and consequently those left fail to make good hearts.

4. Sow Maincrop Carrots and Beet.—Maincrop carrots and beetroot can now be sown. An intermediate or long variety of carrot is usually sown for the maincrop and storage, while small sowings of stump-rooted forms are sown at intervals until July to provide a regular supply of tender young roots.

5. More Sowing of Spinach.—Further sowings of ordinary spinach can be made and New Zealand spinach can now be sown out of doors. It should be given plenty of room, the ultimate plants being spaced out 2 ft. by 3 ft. Sow a few seeds 2 ft. apart in rows 3 ft. apart, and when germinated reduce to one. The plant is vigorous and strong, and leaves and the tips of the shoots can be gathered from the same plants over a long period.

6. Fertilize and Hoe.—A light sprinkling of general fertilizer may be given to crops now well established, particularly the earlier onions. Hoe frequently amongst the crops to work in the fertilizer and to keep down weeds which begin to grow apace at this time of the year. It is important not to destroy them as their competition is felt keenly by young plants. In the later stages they do not matter quite so much, provided they are not allowed to flower and produce seed.

7. Sow Peas.—The final sowing of tall peas should be made now to get full benefit from them.

8. Attend to Fruit.—In the fruit garden suckers may be showing at the base of fruit trees. They should be cut out immediately, as they rob the tree of food. If the season is dry many of the trees and bushes may need watering, particularly on light soils. Wall fruits demand the closest attention in this respect. Apples and pears should

◀ Mr. MIDDLETON says : *Thin out surplus seedings early,*

be given their last spray with lime-sulphur (1 in 100) or Bordeaux, to control scab disease, as soon as the flower petals have fallen. Feed raspberries with fertilizer or liquid manure.

MAY—4th WEEK

1. Plant Mid-Season Leeks.—Leeks for use up to Christmas may now be planted. Do not plant many, as there is so much other produce available at the time. Their greatest value is from Christmas to May. For ordinary purposes the best method of planting is to make holes with a pole or blunt dibber some 6-in. deep. The distance apart should be 12 in. between the rows and 9 in. between the holes. Use only good plants, the roots trimmed a little and the leaves cut back, and drop them in the holes. A little soil can be pushed in to cover the roots, and this should be followed by watering to settle them into position. The holes should not be filled with soil, but left to give room for the leek stems to swell.

2. Kohl Rabi Instead of Turnips.—Kohl rabi should now be sown; it is a useful vegetable for dry, light soil where turnips do not succeed well. It is grown in the same way as turnips in drills 12 in. apart, thinned to 6 in. A fairly rich soil suits it best, and it should not be allowed to grow too large and coarse. Use when of tennis-ball size.

3. Sow for Various Successions.—Successional sowings of radish, shorthorn carrots, six-week turnips, lettuce, etc., should be made according to family requirements and the capacity of the garden. Swede turnips sown now or a little earlier in the north have time to develop to a useful size for winter storage. In the south any sown now will be for autumn use. The storage crop can be sown in June. Earlier sowings of all these crops should be thinned. Both the curled variety and the *Batavian Endive* can be sown now in boxes in a house or frame for transplanting later.

4. Outdoor Tomatoes, Marrows and Cucumbers.—In sheltered gardens of

Turnip Flea Beetle (enlarged)

the south outdoor tomatoes can be planted. Elsewhere it is better to wait a week. There are many places where they will thrive in the open garden, but the position should not be wind-swept. In more difficult areas they should be grown against a wall or fence facing south. In the north they can be planted under cloches. Special tomato cloches can be obtained, and the plants should be grown in trenches 10-in. wide and 10-in. deep to give extra room for growth. Vegetable marrows, too, can be planted out of doors when frost is passed. Seeds may be sown outside, and it is usual to put in three seeds a few inches apart and covered with a sheet of glass. When germinated reduce to one.

Cucumbers can be planted in a cold frame or in a cold house. They will do better in the house if a hot bed is made up for them. Plant in the way already explained.

5. Look to Your Grapes.—Bunches of grapes, which will be developing rapidly, should be thinned out before the fruits become crowded. Use long, thin scissors and hold up the fruits with a stick. Do not use the fingers. Begin at the base of the bunch and work upwards. The border should be given good soakings with water when necessary. The same applies to all wall fruit both inside and out. Stone fruit benefit from a watering with lime water.

6. General Work.—Autumn-fruiting raspberries cut down earlier will have produced growths long enough to need tying to the wire supports. Clean sea-kale beds, and dress with agricultural salt. Mulch peas and other crops on light soil. Earth-up potatoes.

before the roots get tangled, or you may injure those left behind. ▶

JUNE—*1st* WEEK

1. Train Cucumbers.—Cucumbers need frequent training if they are not to get out of hand, no matter where they are grown. All growths should be pinched at each second joint and regularly tied in.

In frames the growths should be pinched in the same way, though the growths are not tied in to any wires or canes. Damping down of the foliage is important; it not only encourages better growth, but checks red-spider mite, which is an enemy of cucumbers and which dislikes damp.

2. Get Tomatoes Out.—Where tomatoes are being grown in large pots for outside culture they can now be moved outside with reasonable safety. Stand in rows in a sheltered spot. Have a strong cane in each pot up which to train the plant and tie all the canes to wire, set some 3 ft. above ground and fastened to stout posts. The others, which are to be grown in the ground, should be planted out carefully. Each plant needs an adequate stake. Better results are obtained if one flower truss is showing or is set. Some growers pinch out the growing point and train up two side shoots. This gives a double-stemmed plant, which is normally very successful.

3. Watch Onions for Seeding.—Autumn-sown onions and those grown from sets often tend to run to seed. As each flower head is seen it should be snapped off. Quite reasonable bulbs will be produced, and these will come in very useful for the early part of the winter.

4. Beware of These Pests.—Broad beans are attacked by an aphis known as black fly, which can cause havoc to a crop in an epidemic year. To check it the soft tips of the plants are pinched out while the plants are in full flower. This tip is the point where infection generally starts, so nip it out as soon as the petals have fallen from the lower flowers and tiny beans are showing. Turnip-flea beetle is an increasing pest. These tiny beetles attack seedling turnips and also brassica seedlings, biting holes in the leaves and sometimes completely destroying the crop. As soon as tiny holes show in the leaves dust the rows with derris powder. It is possible to trap the creatures by using small boards with sticky material on them and making them into a sort of sledge to push over the rows. The pusher stands well back and uses a long handle, so that it is the sledge which disturbs the beetles. They immediately jump and are caught. The beetle is most destructive in dry periods. A light dressing of sulphate of ammonia, followed by a good watering, will keep the plants growing faster than the beetles can destroy them.

5. Sweet Corn, and Strawberries.—Sweet corn can now be planted out in the open. Allow 2 ft. by 2 ft. The more sheltered the spot the better the chances of success. Strawberries should now be netted up to protect the fruits from birds. Bird scarers are not very effective. Slugs have a partiality for the fruits, too, and may be trapped by putting down cabbage leaves for them to congregate under (they must be examined daily), or poisoned by using a mixture of powdered *Meta* tablets and

◀ Mr. MIDDLETON says : *Be prepared for pests and get*

bran. An alternative to bran, which is rather scarce, is dried blood.

6. Sow, Plant and Hoe.—The hoe should be used regularly in the garden to keep down weeds and to prevent them flowering and seeding. Plant out marrows. Sow climbing French beans and scarlet runners. Feed crops with fertilizers, especially onions. When picking gooseberries, leave some to ripen for dessert use.

JUNE—2nd WEEK

1. Look to Tomatoes.—Outdoor tomatoes should now be growing satisfactorily. Those under cloches should be aired during the warmest parts of the day by spacing out the covers. The others will need tying as they grow, and to have all side shoots removed. Those with two stems can have both stems tied to one stake. Too much watering can produce poor rooting conditions and even root rot. Sometimes a mild frost will occur as late as this. It may do some damage, but plants will usually grow away from it.

Continue to train indoor tomatoes correctly. Prevent an overgrowth of side shoots. Allow plenty of ventilation to assist the setting of the fruits. Gentle damping down of the plants each day about noon helps pollenation considerably. Keep an eye open for tomato-mildew attacks. Pale yellow areas first show on the upper surface of the leaves, followed soon by the appearance of the mould on the lower surface, at first yellow and then turning dark brown. Good ventilation helps to prevent it, but when it occurs spray with Shirlan A.G. (salicylanilide) $2\frac{1}{2}$ ounces in 10 gallons of water.

2. Fill Frames.—Frames which have been cleared of seedlings should not be allowed to be idle. It is a good idea to fill them with self-blanching celery. Plants raised from seeds sown inside earlier can be set out 12 in. apart. They will grow up together and blanch each other, and do not need earthing up. They should be ready in September, and can be cleared if the frame is needed.

Broccoli for maturing next spring can now be planted.

3. Puddle Brassicas.—When brassicas of any sort are put out during dry weather it is advisable to puddle the roots. Make a thick mixture of water and clay and dip the roots in it so that it sticks to them, then plant. On land suffering from club root, lime can be added to the mixture and this will help to keep the plant healthy.

4. Runner Beans as Bushes.—If a large number of scarlet runner beans are grown, or if stakes are not available, you can grow them as bushes. They are planted in a single row and the tops pinched off when the plants are about 2 ft. high. This helps them to become bushy. The pods are never so long or straight as on trained plants, but they are worth while.

5. Feed and Plant Out Cucumbers.—Cucumbers can be given an occasional feed with liquid manure. Once a week would be often enough. Ridge cucumbers raised inside can now be planted out. They will grow successfully on soil heaps. They are also useful for cold-frame culture.

6. Look to Next Year's Strawberries.—Select good strawberry plants from which to save runners. One-year-old plants generally give the best results. Do not save from any plants showing signs of disease. Ground beetles often show a partiality for strawberry fruits. They like raw meat even better, so it is possible to trap them by putting a little at the bottom of a glass jar and sinking this to the brim in the soil. It should be examined regularly. Ground beetles or *Carabids* are beneficial insects in other ways and must not be destroyed unnecessarily.

7. General Work.—It will now be possible to begin thinning the fruits of the earliest plums. Earth-up potatoes, first applying fertilizer. Pickling onions may still be sown. Continue to build up the compost heap. Stake Brussels sprouts in windy places. Look out for woolly aphis.

there first. Don't wait until the crops are running alive. ▶

JUNE—3rd WEEK

1. Careful with the Watering-Can !—Where watering is necessary it should be done with care. Remember that once a plant is artificially watered it becomes dependent on such supplies. Do not water until you must, and then give a thorough soaking.

2. Finish Asparagus.—The cutting of asparagus should now be finished. To go on any longer only exhausts the plants. Run strings around the beds fastened to canes or stakes to provide some support for the stems which grow up. Give the asparagus bed a dressing of fertilizer or water with a liquid manure. After cutting is finished it may be necessary to spray the haulms with lead arsenate to control asparagus beetle.

3. Wage War on Pests.—Keep a watch for any pests on the various crops and deal with them as soon as seen. Do not regard them as an act of God which must be suffered in silence. Watch for caterpillars on cabbage and other brassicas. There are normally two broods of these in the year, one in early summer, the other in September. As soon as white butterflies begin to hover among your crops, search for the eggs. Destroy as many as you can before they hatch. The eggs of the large cabbage white butterfly are easy to see. They are normally underneath the leaves, are laid in clutches of 100, and are bright yellow. The eggs of the smaller white butterflies are laid singly, but these are not usually so prolific.

4. Celery, Beans and Cauliflower.—Celery which is growing well should be fed with liquid manure and soot water. Dust old soot over the foliage to keep away the celery fly. Remove side shoots growing from the base of the plants. Broad beans should be pinched, as recommended earlier, to discourage black-fly attacks. Should black-fly appear, spray with nicotine. A dressing of general fertilizer can be hoed in around the plants. Some of the earliest cauliflowers will begin to head up. Cover

CABBAGE-CATERPILLAR AND EGGS

the heads by breaking a leaf and bending it over them.

5. Celeriac and Tomatoes.—Feed celeriac with liquid manure. They require a rich soil and much feeding. Tomatoes planted in the greenhouse now should give fruit well into winter.

6. Sow Final Carrots : Plant Leeks and Broccoli.—Make another sowing of short-horn carrots. This will probably be the last in the north, as sowings after June are rarely successful. Plant leeks as required. Plant broccoli, such as *May Queen* and *Leamington*. These have a passable chance of surviving the winter in the north, if not too big and soft before the bad weather arrives. Much depends on the situation of the garden and the severity of the winter.

7. Top - Dress Cucumbers. — The larger cucumbers growing inside should be top-dressed. The mounds in which they are growing will become permeated with roots, and the time to apply a top-

◀ Mr. MIDDLETON says : *True gardeners never enjoy the*

dressing is when these show through the surface. Make a rich mixture of loam, leaf-mould, sand and fertilizer, and put on a thickness of an inch or two. Firm well with the palms of the hands.

8. Nurse Raspberries and Other Berries.—Pull out any large weeds showing between raspberries, currants, etc. Reduce the number of suckers thrown up by the raspberries to enough to provide growths for next year. Six or seven per plant is usually adequate. Taking out the unnecessary ones at this stage assists the development of those left. Growths of autumn-fruiting raspberries, such as *Lloyd George*, should be thinned to six or seven per plant. Tie the growths of blackberries, loganberries, and any of the various hybrid berries. Water with liquid manure and give a mulch of organic matter to cover the soil. Layer strawberry runners of the plants picked out last week if ready. Take only the first growth on each runner and peg it down, either direct into the soil or into a small pot filled with soil. Plunge the pots into the earth to save watering. Remove any unwanted runners.

9. Thin Out Fruit Trees.—Apples shed a proportion of their fruits naturally, and this is termed the June drop. Begin to thin apple fruit after it. In good seasons Nature's thinning is not enough to relieve the trees of all they should lose. If left unthinned they yield a large crop of small fruits. Remove any diseased or malformed fruits first. In years of poor cropping this is all you need to do. In bumper years make further thinning.

JUNE—4th WEEK

1. Routine Work.—Hoe and weed regularly to reduce unnecessary competition with your crops. Control insect pests. Watch for any diseases such as tomato mildew, onion mildew, etc. Give crops such as runner beans a mulch of leaves or grass mowings to protect them in dry weather.

2. Leeks and Celery.—Water leeks in dry weather, and feed with liquid manure. Exhibitors often bore a separate hole beside each plant into which to put the liquid food. Treat celery the same. They, too, require much liquid nourishment. If slugs appear, water with one of the proprietary slug killers, or put down a mixture of *Meta* and bran, or *Meta* and dried blood.

3. Attack Celery Pests.—As a preventive of leaf blight or rust on celery, spray with Bordeaux mixture about once a fortnight. Signs of attack are brown patches on the leaves, with tiny black spots on them. Do not confuse it with the attacks of celery fly, the larvæ of which is a leaf miner and which eats inside the tissues of the leaf. The appearance of the damage is similar, but the young grub can be seen.

4. Broad Beans and Runners.—When in flower, runner beans can be syringed with water occasionally. This helps the pods to set, as sometimes the flowers drop off. If broad beans have been attacked badly with black fly, spray persistently with nicotine and soft soap. It is essential to hit the insect to kill, so the spray must be carefully applied.

5. Wage War on Caterpillars.—If cabbage caterpillars hatch out and begin to eat the leaves, hand-pick them off if possible. Spray the plants with derris wash. Derris is poisonous to cold-blooded animals such as caterpillars, but not to humans, but if the cabbages are used soon after spraying they should be well washed before cooking.

Sweet corn should be given a dressing of general fertilizer or watered with liquid manure.

6. Sow for Salad Successions.—Keep up succession of salads by making regular sowings. Lettuce must be sown outside, and thinned instead of being planted out. Radish should be sown thinly so that each seedling has a chance to swell. When sown thickly they prevent each other from producing good eatable roots. Mustard and cress can also be obtained from sowings made outside.

fruits of their labours unless they can share them with others. ▶

7. Look to Potatoes, Onions, Leeks. —Earth-up potatoes as they require it. Draw the soil well up to a steep-pointed ridge. This has a tendency to turn away from the tubers the spores of blight which may drop from the foliage. Feed onions weekly now. They should be growing rapidly. Autumn-sown onions will soon begin to swell and should be available for use in August. Earliest leeks will need blanching now. A little soil can be drawn around those in trenches. Those in holes will not need such attention till later. Exhibition leeks are better blanched by tying a 3-in. strip of brown paper around the base before the soil is drawn up. Other strips are added later, as necessary. Make a late sowing of parsley for winter use.

8. Protect Cucumbers. —Cucumbers growing in frames and glasshouses should be well shaded from the sun, otherwise their leaves will be scorched. Whitewash applied to the glass is excellent. There is a special proprietary powder available for the work known as Summer Cloud, which has the advantage of being easy to remove.

9. Take Care of Fruit. —Spray for aphis where necessary, and if caterpillars are attacking gooseberries, spray with derris. Keep up a preliminary thinning of fruits.

JUNE—5th WEEK

1. Gather Beans. —The earliest dwarf French beans will now be ready for picking. They should be gathered while young and tender and not left to get stiff and stringy. It is important to keep them gathered as they become ready, then the plants will keep on bearing more. If allowed to remain and mature, the plant will throw all its energy into the development of seeds rather than producing fresh pods. When runner beans have grown to the top of their stakes the growing point should be pinched off. The bush-grown ones are kept regularly pinched. As pods develop give water, or feed with liquid manure.

2. Shallots and Garlic. —In the south, shallots will be ripening where planted early in February. The soil should be pulled away from the cloves a little to assist ripening. Hoe gently between the rows of garlic, as these will soon be ready for harvesting.

3. Sow Corn Salad. —Though normally sown in August, corn salad or lamb's lettuce can be sown now. A small sowing is advisable. Sow in

For methods to destroy these and other pests, see Encyclopædia

COMMON SNAIL   PEA WEEVIL

◀ Mr. MIDDLETON says : *Hygiene in the garden is important.*

drills 6 or 8 in. apart and thin later to 6 in. They can be sown broadcast if desired.

4. Liquid Manure.—Growing sea-kale will benefit from a soaking of liquid manure. The best liquid manure is obtained from the collecting tank, normally found in any farmyard. This is very strong and rich and needs to be diluted, about a pint to each two-gallon can of water. Failing this, make up your own liquid by filling a sack with manure and suspending it in a tub of water. Other forms of liquid manure can be made by dissolving fertilizers in water.

5. Sow Endive and Radish.—Sow moss-curled endive now to provide an autumn crop. Put the seeds in boxes, in a frame, or on a seed-bed to be transplanted later. When ready set them out at 12 in. each way. The moss-curled type is usually preferred to the Batavian for autumn and early winter use. Make successional sowings of radish to keep up the supply. The long, white form known as *White Icicle* can be sown now for autumn use.

6. Easy with the New Potatoes !—In the more southerly parts of the country, the earliest potatoes may now be ready. But it is wasteful to start digging them while they are very small. Only take up as many at a time as are needed for immediate use. Other rows of second earlies and maincrop should be earthed-up as they need it. Regular earthing is most needed where potatoes have been planted as a cleaning crop on land dug for the first time. Potatoes are a good cleaning crop, not so much by virtue of their habit of growth, but because of the cultural operations they need. Incidentally, it should not be necessary to water potatoes. Some amateurs, while using the hose pipe on their beans and peas, think it does good to soak everything in the garden. This is a mistake. Maincrop carrots should be given a light dressing of general fertilizer, which should be hoed in.

7. Plant Maincrop Leeks.—In the north the main planting of leeks should be made now. It is important to plant in June so as to obtain adequate growth before the winter closes down. It is not generally practicable, therefore, to plant after another crop, such as peas, as can be done in the south, and so a piece of the garden must be set aside for them specially. It is important that good big plants be put out, and these should not have been left so long in the seed rows as to check each other. If they have had a check they may run to seed early. Make another sowing of white turnips and dwarf French beans.

8. Fruit Needs Attention.—Summer pruning of wall fruit and other trained forms can begin. Plums and sweet cherries are done first, and pears soon after. Morello cherries, peaches and nectarines are not summer pruned, except to thin out some of the surplus young shoots which shade the fruit. Water layered strawberry runners when necessary. If silver leaf disease shows on plums, peaches or cherries it must be dealt with. Affected branches must be cut out. When cut a brown stain will be seen in the wood, and the branch must be pruned back a section at a time, until this stain has disappeared.

Do not allow rubbish to accumulate, except on the compost heap. ▶

JULY

JULY—1st WEEK

July is a busy month in the garden even though the bulk of seed-sowing and planting is done. It is the time, too, when the vegetable garden normally looks its best, being filled with maturing and growing crops.

1. Fertilize Onions, Leeks, etc.—The last summer dressing of fertilizer is now given and feeding of crops, such as leeks and onions, is carried out. Both appreciate a watering with soot water. The earliest leeks can have their first slight earthing up, particularly if wanted for showing. Leeks for show should have their stems protected with paper. Plants growing in holes will not be ready for earthing. Water onions if weather is dry. Allow to drain a little, then apply liquid manure. *Never apply liquid manure to plants suffering from drought, but first soak them with water.*

2. Sow Turnips ; Uncover Marrows.—Make a sowing of turnips now in the south for storing in the winter. Varieties such as *Golden Ball* or the dark-skinned *Chirk Castle* are excellent. Marrows in frames can be left uncovered.

3. Feed Tomatoes.—Feed outdoor tomatoes. Top-dress those in pots. Top-dress indoor tomatoes. Good soil, preferably from well-rotted turf, should be mixed with sand and peat, and impregnated with fertilizer as a top-dressing for tomatoes and cucumbers.

4. Work on Celery.—Spray celery and celeriac with weak paraffin emulsion to ward off celery fly. Finish planting main crop of celery.

5. French Beans, Mint and Tarragon.—Make last sowing of dwarf French beans outside. These will mature in September. Make new beds of mint and tarragon by transplanting young growths from old beds. Hoe regularly to keep down weeds.

6. On the Potato Patch.—Spray potatoes with Bordeaux mixture to prevent blight. Lift early potatoes as required. Lifting will now begin in the north where planted out early enough. Fill land cleared of potatoes with winter greens, or sow mustard to dig in as a green manure. Short-horn carrots can also be sown after potatoes.

7. Sowing and Planting.—Sow coleworts for August and September planting, *Rosette* variety for early use, *Hardy Green* for winter. Plant out winter greens. In the north this should be done without delay. Plant white and purple sprouting broccoli, late Savoys, cottager's kale and *January King* cabbage. Plant leeks after early peas in the south. Every delay in planting in the north reduces chances of real success. Sow perpetual spinach (spinach beet) in drills 18 in. apart, and pinches of seed at 9 in. Lift shallots if ready. The foliage will turn brown and die down.

8. Fruit Culture. — Continue to summer-prune trained fruit trees, first doing cherries, plums, pears and then apples. Red currants and gooseberries should also have their growths tipped. The smaller forms of trees are pruned now, not the standard and half-standard forms. Give apple fruits their final thinning. Leave no more than two together at each cluster. With closely-spurred trees, one to each spur is usual. Plums and gages should also be thinned, particularly in bumper years. The earliest cherries on walls will be ripening

◀ Mr. MIDDLETON says : *Six good apples are better than*

in the south. Cover with fish netting to protect from birds. Other wall fruit should be given a good soaking as required. If red spider mite is present, spray with Summer Volck. The mites' presence can be noted by a yellowing and mottling of the foliage. A dull, unhealthy look comes over the leaves. Closer inspection will show the red mites running about just visible to the naked eye. Damping down discourages them, but spraying must be resorted to when they have got a hold.

JULY—2nd WEEK

1. Lift Shallots ; Plant Leeks.—Lift shallots when ready. They should be permitted to mature completely, the foliage dying right down. When thoroughly ripe lift and turn the roots up to the sun for a day or so, and dry off thoroughly. Continue planting leeks in the south.

2. Thin Rows of Seedlings.—Any crops sown in June, such as carrots, turnips, beet or lettuce, will need to be thinned out to the required distances apart.

3. Sow Spring Cabbage in North.—In the more northern parts of the country the first spring cabbage should now be sown. In the midlands and south it is too early, as they will either run to seed or heart up before Christmas.

4. Plant Winter Greens.—Make successional sowings of lettuce, radish, and spinach. Sow as intercrops between late-planted greens. Sow Batavian endive either in boxes or a frame to be transplanted outside when ready. The Batavian is better than the curled forms for late work.

5. Lift Potatoes.—Lift early potatoes as required. Select suitable ones for seed if the stock was new this year. Do not expose to the light for some time yet. Put in a cool place.

6. Fertilize and Water Peas.—Give tall peas a dressing of general fertilizer, or mix one up of superphosphate and sulphate of potash. Water in dry weather. Peas which are podding up

should be watered to help the pods to swell. Pull out any large weeds showing in the rows.

7. Sow Parsley.—Make a late sowing of parsley. This will be suitable for winter use. It is a good idea to sow in a rectangular patch, so that a wooden frame can be placed round and covered with a light in bad weather.

8. Hunt Caterpillars.—Caterpillars on cabbages if not destroyed should not be allowed to eat their fill and prepare to pupate. Otherwise a fresh batch of butterflies will emerge in August and another brood of caterpillars will attack your plants in the autumn. The caterpillars, when they have eaten enough, crawl to walls and fences, climb up them and turn into a pupa or chrysalis. These, if seen, should be destroyed.

9. Pick Broad Beans.—Pick broad beans as ready. Any of the early sowings which are finished should be pulled up. Chop the stems and place on compost heap. Save a few to use for trapping earwigs when they attack fruit.

10. Examine and Prune Fruit Trees, and Destroy Pests.—Fruit trees which have been grafted should be examined to see the grafts have not loosened. Carry on with summer pruning, cutting back apple laterals to five or six leaves. The main leader growth is not touched. Spray with nicotine for green fly if there are signs of it on the trees. Spray apples with lead arsenate to control codlin moth. Remove suckers from wall fruit. Protect Morello cherries from bird attacks. Pick and use for cooking and preserve some for winter use. Tie sack bands around trunks of trees to trap apple blossom weevil and codlin moth. These pests hibernate about now and the bands provide a suitable place. Leave until November, then burn them. Branches of plums and cherries, heavily laden with fruit, should be propped to prevent breaking. Layer strawberry runners as necessary. Remove nets when fruit is gathered and use to protect raspberries. Cut off unwanted runners. Bunch young

twelve half-developed ones. If too many set, thin them out. ▶

Your Cropping

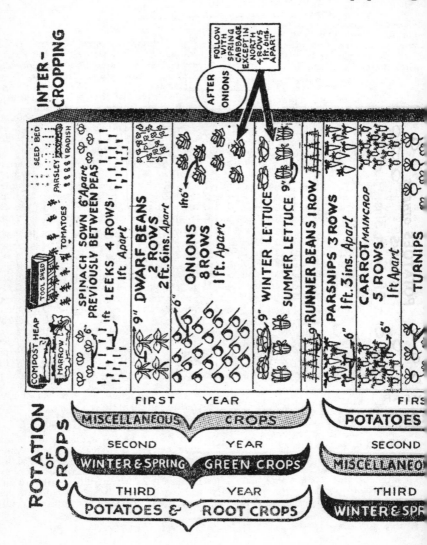

COMPOST HEAP

TOOL SHED

SEED BED

PARSLEY

RADISH

TOMATOES

HARROW

SPINACH SOWN 6"Apart PREVIOUSLY BETWEEN PEAS

LEEKS 4 ROWS 1ft Apart

DWARF BEANS 2 ROWS 2ft.6ins. Apart

ONIONS 8 ROWS 1ft. Apart

AFTER ONIONS

FOLLOW WITH SPRING CABBAGE EXCEPT IN NORTH 4 ROWS 1ft.6ins. APART

WINTER LETTUCE 9"

SUMMER LETTUCE 9"

RUNNER BEANS 1 ROW

PARSNIPS 3 ROWS 1ft.3ins. Apart

CARROT MAINCROP 5 ROWS 1ft Apart

TURNIPS

ROTATION OF CROPS

FIRST YEAR
MISCELLANEOUS CROPS

SECOND YEAR
WINTER & SPRING GREEN CROPS

THIRD YEAR
POTATOES & ROOT CROPS

FIRST
POTATOES

SECOND
MISCELLANEOUS

THIRD
WINTER & SPRING

d Rotation Plan

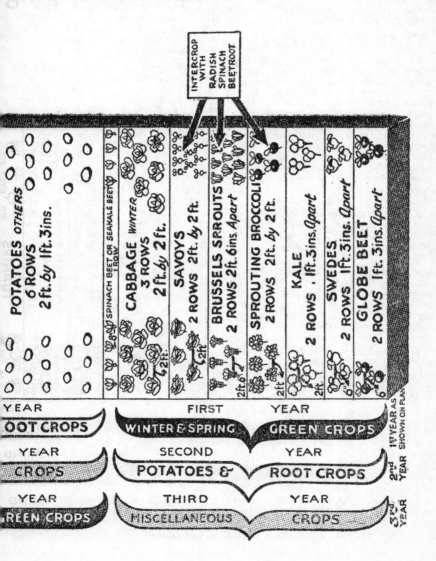

INTER-CROP WITH RADISH SPINACH BEETROOT

POTATOES *OTHERS* 6 ROWS 2ft. by 1ft. 3ins.

SPINACH BEET OR SEAKALE BEET 1 ROW

CABBAGE *WINTER* 3 ROWS 2ft. by 2ft.

SAVOYS 2 ROWS 2ft. by 2ft.

BRUSSELS SPROUTS 2 ROWS 2ft. 6ins. *Apart*

SPROUTING BROCCOLI 2 ROWS 2ft. by 2ft.

KALE 2 ROWS 1ft. 3ins. *Apart*

SWEDES 2 ROWS 1ft. 3ins. *Apart*

GLOBE BEET 2 ROWS 1ft. 3ins. *Apart*

YEAR	FIRST	YEAR	1st YEAR AS SHOWN ON PLAN
OOT CROPS	WINTER & SPRING	GREEN CROPS	
YEAR	SECOND	YEAR	2nd YEAR
CROPS	POTATOES &	ROOT CROPS	
YEAR	THIRD	YEAR	3rd YEAR
REEN CROPS	MISCELLANEOUS	CROPS	

growths of brambles, loganberries and such like together to avoid damage and to ease picking. Control e wigs on peaches and nectarines either by trapping or putting down a poison bait. Use ½ pound sodium fluoride, 4 pounds bran, 1 pint black treacle and 1 gallon water to make the bait.

JULY—3rd WEEK

1. Train Cucumbers.—Stop and train cucumbers as required. Pinch out the growing point after every second leaf. From the first leaf joint allow only one cucumber to develop. From the second joint allow one fruit and the growth bud to develop. The bud grows on and is stopped at the second leaf again. It is tied to wire in the greenhouse, but in the frames is allowed to trail over the soil. Fruits in frames should have a piece of glass placed under them. Ridge cucumbers growing outside will appreciate a feed of liquid manure.

2. Plant Out Broccoli.—Plant out the late-heading broccoli without delay. Puddle the roots if the weather is dry. *Methven's Late June* is a good hardy variety for doubtful areas.

3. Clear Strawberry Beds for Greens. —Strawberry beds which are three years old and have been picked should be cleared and planted with winter greens. There is no need to dig deeply ; a light forking over is adequate, as these greens prefer a firm base.

4. Attack Onion Mildew.—If onion mildew appears (a white fungus on the collar of the young bulbs), pull up badly infected plants and dust remainder of bed with flowers of sulphur.

5. Feed Beet.—Use globe beet as ready. Feed later sown crops. Any that run to seed should have the flower head snapped off and the roots used immediately.

6. Sow Spinach ; Feed Marrows.— Sow perpetual spinach if not already in. It will supply leaves in winter. Thin to one plant at every 9 in. Feed marrows to swell the fruits. Use while small.

The ideal size for table use is when about 12-in. long and while the skin can be penetrated by the thumb nail.

7. More Sowing, Planting and Thinning.—Coleworts sown in late May can be planted out 12 by 15 in. Thin out chicory sown earlier to one every 9 in. Plant late celery without delay. Make a late sowing of dwarf peas in the south to crop in September.

8. Forestall or Destroy Pests.—Keep carrots and celery dusted with old soot. It helps growth of leaf and plant and discourages fly. Watch for slugs and snails and destroy. Other pests must be controlled also. If anything occurs in the way of trouble which you do not understand, get expert advice. Do not accept it as being in the natural course of things.

9. Examine Tomatoes for Disease.— Watch for stripe disease on your indoor tomatoes. This is a virus disease which generally attacks the top of the plant first. It shows itself in black marks down the main stem, and along the leaf stems, and in black marks on the leaves. Fruit in the region of attack becomes blotchy. Cut back plants to well below where the lowest stripes show. Wash the knife immediately afterwards and burn the affected plant parts. Take up a sideshoot to replace the centre. Badly attacked plants should be grubbed up and burned.

10. Sever Strawberries.—Early-layered strawberry runners should now be ready for severing from the parent plant. Those in pots can be stood on ashes or put in a cold frame. Do not allow them to get dry.

11. Cut Out Diseased Fruit Branches. —Cut out branches of plums attacked by silver leaf disease and paint the cut surfaces. Any dead branches in other fruits, e.g., gooseberries, should also be cut out and burned. Complete fruit thinning as soon as possible.

12. Attack Weeds.—Keep weeds in check, and do not let them seed.

◀ **Mr. MIDDLETON** says : *A pot placed over a large dandelion*

JULY—4th WEEK

1. Stop Outdoor Tomatoes.—As soon as outdoor tomatoes are fully grown and are showing the third or fourth truss of flowers, pinch out the growing point, two leaves above the truss. In the south four trusses can be left on each plant, but in the north and cold districts three is enough. Do not pinch out the point immediately above the top truss, but leave two leaves to draw up the sap from the roots and to manufacture food for the fruits.

2. Dress Sprouts, Seakale, Beans, Celery.—Give Brussels sprouts a dressing of general fertilizer or of sulphate of ammonia alone. This encourages leaf development. Feed seakale with liquid manure to build up the crowns for next winter. Water runner beans as required. These, too, appreciate liquid manure. Self-blanching or other celery in frames should be watered and fed.

3. Sow Spring Cabbage.—In the far north make second sowing of spring cabbage, in the north and midlands make main sowing, and in the south make early sowing. The best time for your district can be found by experiment or by asking local gardeners. Make two sowings with ten to fourteen days between them. Where only a limited number can be grown, make only the late sowing in the first week in August. Seeds put in a few days too early may result in plants which run to seed. There are many varieties to choose from, and on this point local advice is usually the most reliable.

4. Treat Lanky Artichokes.—If Jerusalem artichokes have become very tall and there is danger of them blowing over, cut off a foot or so at the top.

5. Onions, Final Stages.—Autumn-sown onions, such as *White Italian* and *White Lisbon*, should soon be ready for lifting. When ripe, bend over the foliage and loosen root-hold by easing slightly with a fork. After about a week lift and expose roots to sun, dry off and take inside. These should be used from now and not stored for long.

6. Sow Radishes and Endive ; Thin Salsify.—Sow *Black Spanish* and *China Rose* radishes in drills 12 in. apart. Thin out later. These varieties are large-rooted ones which can be stored and used during winter. If you have not done so already, thin salsify and scorzonera to 6–9 in. apart. Sow endive for succession.

7. Fill Vacant Space.—Fill any vacant space, including any blanks which have arisen in earlier batches of winter greens, with late greens or leave for spring cabbage, occupying it with salads in the meantime.

8. Spray Potatoes.—Spray potatoes again with Bordeaux mixture to cover newly-grown foliage. Give at least two preventative sprays in areas where the disease usually occurs. If desired, the Bordeaux mixture can be bought as a dust and applied to the plants by means of bellows. Burgundy mixture can also be used.

9. Care for Fruit.—Thin out the growths of gooseberries to assist the ripening of the wood. Where American gooseberry mildew has been a nuisance, feed the bushes with potash and phosphates. The very earliest apples will soon be ready, varieties such as *Irish Peach* and *Beauty of Bath*. Pick and use as ready, do not put for storage. Any very old fruit bushes which are fruiting badly should be grubbed out after fruiting and replaced later by young ones. This is worth while in the long run even if it means the loss of a certain amount of fruit for a year or so. If room is available young bushes can be planted in a new position and the old ones left until these are established before being pulled up. Water autumn-fruiting raspberries.

10. Preserve Fruit.—Preserve any surplus fruit either by jamming or bottling. Preserving with sugar syrup is best, but it can be done with water only where sugar is not available.

plant will blanch it white, and turn it into a delicious salad. ▶

AUGUST

AUGUST—1st WEEK

1. Use Onions.—Use autumn-sown onions as soon as ready. Do not leave them in the soil until they begin to split.

2. Sow Cabbage, Spinach and Lettuce. —Make the main sowing of spring cabbage on seed bed. This sowing will not run to seed so readily as earlier ones. Where they will not be planted out until late September or October it pays to prick out the seedlings 6 by 6 in., into frames or a spare piece of the garden. This avoids a check and produces fine plants. Sow winter or prickly spinach. Seeds can either be spaced out or sown thinly in a drill. Sow lettuce in cold frame for late use. They should be suitable for planting out at the end of the month. Thin out perpetual spinach sown earlier to one seedling every 9 in. Planting of later greens is still possible in south.

3. Earth-up Celery.—Earth-up the earliest celery. Do it gradually, covering about 3 in. of stem at a time. Earth at fortnightly intervals. Mix a little naphthalene with the soil to discourage slugs. Water for celery blight, and spray with Bordeaux mixture at first sign of it.

4. Sow Onions.—Sow onions now for next year's early crop. Choose a sheltered spot where they can winter in the open. In districts where there is risk of loss in winter sow in such a way that it will be possible to erect a temporary frame over them. For example, sow five rows 1-ft. apart and as long as you have lights to cover. Later, put boards down the sides and at the end, and cover with lights. Temporary frames such as this are extensively used by professional gardeners. That is why a surplus number of lights is so useful. Experience shows that plants such as these onions will thrive quite satisfactorily until Christmas, and then succumb quickly, unless they are given a little protection during severe weather. Cloches, of course, can be used. Turnips for a supply of leaves in spring should be sown now.

5. Help on Tomatoes.—Increase water supply to tomatoes in cold house as they grow bigger and the border fills with roots. The earliest greenhouse tomatoes in the southern parts will now be over. They should be taken out and the house can be planted with cucumbers. Tomatoes growing out of doors are sometimes attacked by potato blight. It will pay to give these a protective spraying with Bordeaux mixture.

6. Prune Blackcurrants.—Blackcurrants which have been picked clear of fruit should be pruned. The fruit is borne on last year's wood, and all the pruning necessary is to cut out the old branches which have borne the fruit. Cutting out the oldest in this way encourages the development of the young branches from the bottom, which will bear next year's fruit.

7. Destroy Wasp Nests.—Watch for wasps attacking wall fruit. Study their flight away from the fruit and you will be able to trace them to their nests and destroy them.

8. Dig New Strawberry Bed.—Prepare new strawberry bed by digging deeply, two spits if time allows, and incorporating some manure and bone

◀ Mr. MIDDLETON says : *Dwarf French beans are nicest*

meal. Clean up existing beds. Cut off unwanted runners.

9. Attack Fruit Pests.—Spray apple trees for woolly aphis, if present. Use nicotine with a good spreader and aim at the infected parts. Trap earwigs attacking wall fruit. Use inverted plant pots with straw in them, or pieces of broad-bean stem.

10. Sow Corn Salad.—Sow corn salad (lamb's lettuce) in drills, 12 in. apart.

AUGUST—2nd WEEK

1. Feed Tomatoes.—Feed tomatoes as necessary. Those growing well inside and carrying a lot of fruit will want a dressing about once a week. Vary the feeding somewhat. One week use general fertilizer, next liquid manure, next a proprietary fertilizer such as Clay's, which is excellent ; and so on. Give at least two top-dressings. When the border or trough is so filled with roots that they show on the surface, put on a ½-in. layer of specially mixed soil, enriched by fertilizers. Firm this with a rammer or blunt piece of wood. Use a rose on the watering-can for a day or two until settled. Do not completely fill border with soil, or water will run off before it can soak through. The same procedure is necessary with those grown in pots. These, too, should be left ½-in. or so to hold water. Tomatoes sown earlier for winter use may be ready for potting. Move into 3½-in. size.

2. Sow, Harvest and Protect Onions.—Sow onions if not done. Suitable varieties are *White Lisbon, Grant Zittau, Giant Rocca,* and *Giant Tripoli.* Harvest pickling onions when ready. Dry off and pickle as soon as possible. Any onions growing on the bed which are going thick-necked and not bulbing properly should have their leaves bent over at the neck or as near to it as possible to check growth. Pull up and use as required. They should not be stored, as they do not keep, but if harvested later with the better ones, should be put for early use.

3. Lift Beetroot.—Lift globe beetroot that is ready and put in temporary

store. A covering of soil is enough to keep them fresh. If left in the ground they become coarse.

4. Stake Peas.—Peas sown last month should be staked unless they are dwarf varieties.

5. Earth-up Celery. — Use crops grown beside the celery trench and begin to earth-up a little. The very late ones will not be ready yet.

6. Sow and Thin Radish and Cabbage.—Thin winter radish and make another sowing if required. Make second sowing of spring cabbage if not yet done. Prick out those sown in July so as to avoid a check.

7. Preserve Beans.—Any surplus dwarf beans or runner beans should be picked and preserved in salt. They should be shredded, not cut into lumps, placed in an earthenware jar and put down in layers. Salt is dressed on each layer. About 1 pound of salt to 3 pounds of beans is sufficient.

8. Complete Summer Pruning.—Complete summer pruning of fruit trees as soon as possible, so as to help ripen the fruit, to expose the wood to the sun and ripen that also, and to concentrate food into the base of the growth for encouraging the development of spurs. Prune blackcurrants as fruit is cleared.

9. Clean up Strawberry Beds, and Make New Ones.—Clean up strawberry beds, removing dead leaves and straw and forking between the plants. Where mite is a nuisance it is sometimes beneficial to fire the straw before cleaning up. This burns the foliage of the plants but does them no real harm. Prepare new strawberry bed as opportunity offers. Look after young plants which will be needed to fill it. If strawberries are to be grown in frames, pot on some of the runners into 3½-in. pots. Keep shaded for a day or two until recovered.

10. Don't Water Peaches !—Peaches and nectarines which are ripening should not be fed, and watering should be omitted where possible, as the fruit is easily spoiled. Pick as it ripens.

when about five inches long, cooked whole without slicing. ▶

11. **Late-sown Beet, in the South,** should be singled to 6-in. apart. Spray Cabbage with Nicotine if Aphis Appears.

AUGUST—3rd WEEK

1. **Watch for Mildew.**—Watch for mildew on peas. If it comes at the end of a crop, when most of the pods are picked, pull up the plants. Should it be sooner, dust with flowers of sulphur.

2. **Prick Out Cabbage.**—Prick out spring cabbage now ready. It may be necessary to protect them from birds, so put wire netting or black cotton over the plants.

3. **Earth-up and Feed Leeks.**—Earth-up early leeks. The show specimens will be almost completed now. Feed other leeks occasionally, especially with liquid manure.

4. **Sow and Plant Endive.**—Make a last sowing of Batavian endive outside and prick out later into frames. In any event they will have to be moved into frames later or at least given cloche protection. Plant out moss-curled endive 12 in. apart.

5. **Feed Marrows and Asparagus.**—Feed marrows with liquid manure. Use the fruits while young and soft. Feed asparagus similarly.

6. **Harvest Haricot Beans.**—The earliest haricot beans will soon be ready for harvesting. When the pods have turned brown, the plants should be pulled up, tied in bunches, and hung head downwards in an open shed or room.

7. **Harvest, Protect and Prune Fruit.**—When the peaches and nectarines have been gathered, prune out the old fruiting wood. Cut back to where there is a young growth emerging from it. This early pruning helps the young shoots to ripen and mature, and these are the ones which will bear the fruit next year. Pick early pears, such as *Marguerite Marillat*, and store for a few days before use. With pear trees carrying large fruits, minimise the possibility of damage should winds blow off any of the fruits. Fish nets looped around the bottom in such a way as to catch the fruits are excellent.

8. **Prepare Storage.**—Get the room or loft where you will store your fruit in ship-shape order. Clean down the walls, brush it out, and well ventilate it. Nets no longer needed should be cleaned and stored away. They are precious. During the winter any necessary repairs can be made.

9. **Prune Cherries.**—Morello cherries on walls should be pruned as soon as the fruit is picked. With these the fruited wood is also cut out.

10. **Plant Out Strawberries.**—Plant out strawberry runners on the new bed. Allow 30 in. between the rows and 15 in. between the plants. Make firm, but do not bury the crowns.

11. **Sow Onions Out of Doors ; Sow Prickly Spinach in Rows 12 in. apart ; Plant Out Lettuce ; Use Cauliflowers Before they Bolt.**

AUGUST—4th WEEK

1. **Clear Cucumbers.**—The earlier crops of cucumbers will now be finished and should be cleared out. Water ridge-cucumbers as required.

2. **Feed Seakale and Rhubarb.**—Feed seakale and rhubarb occasionally to build up the crowns. Rhubarb should not be allowed to produce flower stems, as these steal energy, particularly after a frosty winter.

3. **Support Asparagus.**—See that asparagus growths are adequately supported. If any are knocked over and snapped it spoils root development for next year's crop. Usually two strings around the outside of the bed are enough.

4. **Water Peas and Beans.**—Water peas and beans as they require it. The taller forms are most likely to need water, and all sizes benefit when the pods are swelling. It is better to give a thorough soaking once a week than

◀ Mr. MIDDLETON says : *We must try to return to the soil as*

Good clean straw or a strawberry mat should be placed around strawberry plants when in flower. These provide a clean place for fruit to rest on and protect it against pests.

dribble a little on every other day. The weather controls the need for watering, and where there are water restrictions an alternative is to mulch around the plants with leaves, grass mowings or manure. Grass mowings, unfortunately, deteriorate rapidly into an evil-smelling mass unless kept stirred, so if manure is obtainable it is better to use it.

5. Make Cauliflowers Last.—As cauliflowers head up, bend a leaf over them to keep them white and prevent dirt and grit getting in. It is common for a number to head up together, far too many for immediate use. If you do not want to give them away, lift the plants, and either heel in soil in a shed or hang up, heads downwards, under cover. They will keep for a few days this way, and it is better than letting them bolt.

6. Use or Check Onions.—If onions are ready, check a little by placing a fork between the rows and easing the plants up gently. This breaks the roots and encourages ripening. Use thick-necked onions as required.

7. Sow Lettuce.—Sow lettuce in boxes or frame for cloche, cold frame or outdoor culture later on. *All the Year Round* is a good variety. So is *Arctic King*. Cos lettuce, such as *Winter White*, can also be sown now.

8 Last Chance for Onion-Sowing.—This is really the last week in which to sow onions outside. The border chosen for the job should be moderately rich and well prepared ; but not too well or they may grow soft and fail to stand the winter. A piece well-manured for early potatoes is suitable.

9. Prick Out Cauliflowers.—Prick out cauliflower plants into cold frame to over-winter. If the sowing has not been done put some seed in a box. Plants raised thus are good for growing in a cold greenhouse in winter, or even in pots. They can also be over-wintered in a frame and planted in March. Some growers prefer to sow in a warm house in January, as they say they get the crop just as soon.

10. Pick Apples.—Pick apples as ready. These earlier varieties can be gathered slightly under-ripe, when they will mature indoors and make excellent eating. Of course, they must not be too under-ripe or they will merely shrivel up. These varieties should be used fairly soon, as they will not keep. That is why care in the selection of varieties is essential when planting fruit trees. To have too many earlies means an unprofitable glut.

much as we take from it, not only in the chemical sense, but in bulk. ▶

SEPTEMBER

SEPTEMBER—1st WEEK

1. Plant Spring Cabbage.—As soon as land is available begin to plant first spring cabbage in the north. As this crop likes a firm rooting medium there is no need to dig the soil. For instance, when potatoes have been lifted just rake the surface down and plant the cabbage.

2. Sow Cauliflowers. — Sow cauliflowers for spring planting or inside culture if not already done. Put in seeds of two or three different suitable varieties. This avoids the trouble of too many heading up at once. Remember when sowing any of the brassica family that a small packet of seeds will give many plants. One ounce has several thousand seeds in it.

3. Help Onions to Colour up.—Onions which are nearly ready for ripening and which have a rough outer skin could have the skin removed. Rubbed off it exposes the smoother underskin to the sun and helps to colour up. It should be done only a few days before lifting, and only the very loose outer skin should be removed.

4. Remove Dead Leaves from Tomatoes.—If any of the lower leaves on outdoor tomatoes have turned brown or withered, remove them. Healthy green leaves should never be removed or cut back, as this reduces the supply of food needed to swell the fruits. Indoor tomatoes are slightly different as they are grown somewhat crowded together. The bottom trusses of fruit when fully grown can be exposed to the light more by removing some of the lowest leaves and cutting off portions of those which are shading the fruits.

In the ordinary course of things, full leaves should not be removed until they show that their time has come by flagging and turning yellow. This stripping is frequently overdone.

5. Sow Turnips.—Sow turnips in the south for winter or spring greens. Varieties such as *Manchester Market, Greentop Stone,* and *Chirk Castle* are suitable.

6. Case Mushrooms. — Mushroom beds made up earlier, and spawned when the temperature had fallen to 75°–80° F., will now be ready for casing. Put an even layer of soil all over 2 in. thick. A layer of straw over the bed helps to keep the temperature even and protects buttons as they come through. Further beds can be made up to ensure a succession.

7. Put Out Winter Lettuce.—Lettuce sown earlier can be pricked out into a cold frame or, where suitable, planted outside to provide a winter crop.

8. Dig-in Green Manure.—Land sown in summer with mustard for a green manure should be turned over. The mustard is first trodden or rolled down. When dug the ground can be filled with spring cabbage.

9. Beware of Caterpillars.—Do not allow the second brood of cabbage caterpillars to thrive. Spray immediately with derris or a proprietary article containing it.

10. Plant Out Endive.—Plant out endive where it can be given cloche protection or put straight into a cold frame. The lights only need putting on later. Another sowing can be made in boxes for

◀ **Mr. MIDDLETON** says : *Where possible, stable manure should be*

pricking out into frame. They will give a supply after Christmas.

11. Attend to Celery.—Remove side growths from later celery and water well if necessary. The earlier batch will be completely earthed-up, leaving only the top of the leaves showing and will soon be ready for use.

12. Protect Parsley.—Plant some parsley into a frame in districts where it is hard to keep over winter.

13. Easy with Fertilizer on Greens.— Do not feed late winter greens. Those which mature before Christmas, such as certain early broccoli, can have a dressing of fertilizer. Feed celeriac.

14. Thin Out Crops.—Thin out perpetual spinach to 8 in. apart. Thin out other crops needing it, such as turnips. Earth-up leeks ; build up compost heap ; hoe out any weeds showing.

SEPTEMBER—2nd WEEK

1. Sow Cauliflowers Under Cloches.— If desired, cauliflowers can be sown very thinly in a straight drill and covered with cloches. When they come through, thin out to 9 in. apart. It is claimed for this method that they mature much earlier than when planted out. Leave under the cloches all winter. And, by the way, see that your cloches are repaired if any are broken.

2. Advance Tomatoes.—All tomato plants, inside or out, should have their fruit picked as it ripens. The removal of fruit hastens the colouring of the others. Tomatoes grown in large pots out of doors should now be moved into a greenhouse to finish off and ripen.

3. Harvest Onions.—Onions should now be harvested without further delay. They should have their foliage bent over at the neck. This produces a check to growth, and the food in the leaves passes into the bulb which swells perceptibly afterwards. It is important that the leaves be not snapped, so do it gently. Ripening is thus hastened, and after a week or so the bulbs can be lifted. If wet weather sets in, lift fairly soon,

otherwise fresh root-growth may begin and the bulbs soften.

4. Lift and Store Carrots.—Lift maincrop carrots as soon as ready. This is when the foliage has begun to turn yellow or has taken on a dull, metallic appearance. Choose a dry day for the job. Ease them up with a fork if they are a long-rooted variety. Cut off the tops near to the root, and do not wash before storing. Small quantities can be stored in dry sand in boxes. If there is shed accommodation, they can be put in a corner and well covered with sand. Larger quantities should be clamped out of doors. The heap is built up like a pyramid, and straw is placed all around it with the straws running from top to bottom as near as possible. Cover with a 4- or 5-in. layer of earth and pat it down. Leave a tuft of straw sticking from the top as a ventilator.

5. Plant Out and Sow Lettuce.—Plant out winter lettuce in suitable spot in the open. A protected border is ideal. In general this is only worth while in the south and midlands, but there are a few favoured localities in the north where it can be done. Sow lettuce for greenhouse culture. Suitable varieties are *Gotte-a-forcer*, a French variety, and *Cheshunt Early Giant*. Both will grow satisfactorily despite short days and poor light.

6. Gather Peas and Haricots for Drying.—Peas being grown for seed or drying should be pulled up, the haulms tied in bundles and hung in an open shed until the pods can be dealt with. Harvest haricot beans as the pods turn brown and the leaves begin to wither. Treat the same as peas above.

7. Thin Out and Blanch Endive.— Thin out seedling endive sown earlier. Any that are fully grown in the open can be blanched. This is done by completely covering the plant with a box or large pot. You may be recommended to place a slate on the plant, but don't do it, particularly with the moss-curled variety. The slate too often proves

used on heavy land. For light soils use cow or farmyard manure. ▶

attractive to slugs, and in wet weather the endive decays. Use something larger. Do not begin to blanch until the plants are fully grown.

8. Prepare for Fruit Planting.—Prepare for autumn planting of fruit trees and bushes as soon as possible. The digging of the soil should take priority so that it is in good condition for planting. All the area should be dug, double dug if possible. Strong manure is not desirable for young fruit trees, as it has a tendency to cause too much soft tender growth.

9. Thin Spinach.—Thin winter spinach to 8-in. apart.

SEPTEMBER—3rd WEEK

1. Lift Potatoes.—Lift potatoes as soon as ready. Begin with the second-earlies and continue with maincrop. When lifting, push the fork into the sides of the rows, well down, to minimise the risk of piercing the potatoes. Throw them clear of the soil. Leave for an hour or two to dry a little, but do not leave more than a few hours or the sunlight will turn them green. Where the leaves are heavily attacked by blight, cut away the tops first, burn them, and do not lift the potatoes for at least a week. This gives time for the sun to kill any spores which might otherwise infect the potatoes and cause decay in store.

2. Build-up Compost.—As crops are finished remove any remains and rubbish and place on the compost heap. Such things as the hard stems of cabbage should be chopped up. If brassica stumps show signs of clubroot disease, burn them. Diseased potato tops should not be used for compost either.

3. Plant Out Cabbage.—Plant out spring cabbage according to requirements. The second batch can be planted in the north, while in the south the first batch will be ready. It is good to draw out triangular drills 6-in. deep and to put the cabbage at the bottom of them. Planting distances vary a little according to the district, but a usual distance is

18 by 18 in. If you have plenty of plants put them in 12 by 9 in. This provides a reserve in case of loss ; after Christmas, if they thrive, the alternate plants can be removed and used as early greens. Do not leave them all in.

4. Lift and Store Carrots.—Lift carrots and beet in the north and store. In the south there is less urgency. Store in dry sand. They can be put behind a wall or fence and packed between the wall and a board, or they can be stored in barrels or clamps.

5. Earth-up and Protect Celery.—Earth-up celery a little at a time. Mix naphthalene with the soil to discourage slugs. These pests have a habit of eating the outside of the stalks, and the damaged strips turn brown. A very light sprinkling of salt alongside the rows, before earthing-up, helps to keep the celery crisp and sweet. Gather self-blanching celery from frames.

6. If Frost Comes.—Cut all marrows if frost occurs and put them in a cool, airy room to store. They will keep for a considerable time if ripe. Very small immature ones can be used up in the kitchen.

7. Ripen Outdoor Tomatoes.—Tomatoes grown in the open ground should be pulled up by the roots, taken inside as they are, and hung up in the light. Most of the fruit will then colour satisfactorily. It is better than pulling off the individual fruit, though this can be done if desired, and the tomatoes be put in shallow boxes with straw to help them to ripen. Pick them over frequently.

8. Work with the Hoe.—Winter crops should be hoed to keep down the weeds which are usually a nuisance in September. Also hoe between onions sown last month : they will be showing nicely now.

9. Lift Onions.—Lift onions which were bent over earlier, and leave on the surface of the soil, exposing the bases to the sun. When lifting ease out with a fork to avoid tearing the base. In wet weather, or if there is a risk of

◀ **Mr. MIDDLETON** says : *Light sandy soil is improved by adding*

pilfering, take the onions inside and dry off in an airy room or shed.

10. Prepare for Wall Fruit Planting. —If you intend to plant any fruit trees against walls, make up the borders now by deep digging. Put grease-bands around trunks of fruit trees. Continue to dig land for fruit tree and bush planting.

11. Order Manure.—Now is the time to buy manure—farmyard manure for preference—ready for a new round of digging.

SEPTEMBER—4th WEEK

1. Harvest Home !—Crops which are ready should be harvested. To leave them in the ground longer than is necessary lays them open to further attacks from pests, particularly slugs

which are voracious feeders at this time of the year. Deterioration is sure to begin, especially if the weather is cold and wet. Root crops tend to coarsen or to decay. Cut and collect bracken for purposes of protection if you happen to live near where it grows. Store in a shed if possible to keep dry, or stack out of doors and protect from rain.

2. Store Onions.—Onions which have been left on the ground, base upwards, to ripen, should be brought inside after a day or so. They may be tied in bunches of six or seven and hung on sticks arranged horizontally in a shed. Or they can be put in a single layer on a stretch of wire netting, placed anywhere so long as it does not rest on the ground. On sunny days it can be carried outside to finish the ripening. Later, the onions can be fastened in ropes. To do this they are tied with string to a central

THE WHOLE ART OF STORING ROOT CROPS IN CLAMPS

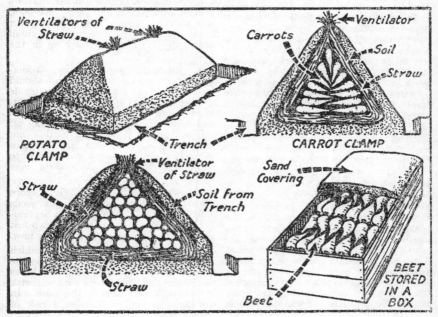

Ventilators of Straw

Carrots — Ventilator

Soil

Straw

POTATO CLAMP

Trench

CARROT CLAMP

Straw

Ventilator of Straw

Soil from Trench

Sand Covering

BEET STORED IN A BOX

Straw

Beet

soft, rotting material such as lawn mowings, to make it spongy. ▶

core of wood or straws. The place to keep onions is in an open shed or hung before the open window of a room. Never keep them in warmth, and never close windows except in very frosty weather.

3. Lift and Store Potatoes.—Continue to lift and store potatoes. There is no need to wait until the tops have died down completely, as the tubers will be mature. In slug- and wireworm-infested soil, the sooner they are lifted the better.

4. Fill Blanks.—Fill vacant pieces of the garden with spring cabbage. Leave some seedlings in a frame to provide spares for filling blanks in spring. This is a wise precaution, particularly in the north. Do not cover with lights until later, when the weather becomes bad.

5. Prick Cauliflowers.—Prick cauliflower seedlings into cold frame as soon as ready. Keep lights on for a day or so, then leave off until the bad weather begins.

6. Gather Tomato Seed.—Trusses of tomato fruits marked for seed and allowed to ripen should be taken off as ready. A box with paper in the bottom should be near each truss in the later stages, as fruits tend to drop off. Mark each box with the name of the variety. Leave them for a little time, and when they are really soft and ripe, wash the seeds away from the flesh. The best way to do it is to make a small sieve of perforated zinc, crush some fruits into it and wash under the tap. Allow the seeds to dry before packeting them.

7. War Against Caterpillars.—The late brood of cabbage caterpillars will now be leaving the plants to pupate, if you have let them get so far. They crawl along the ground until they find a fence or wall up which to climb. They particularly like to snuggle beneath a window ledge, a gutter or a door lintel. They will go right to the top of the house. Hunt them and slay them ! Frequently they are parasitised by the ichneumon fly, which lays its eggs in them while small. From these, tiny grubs hatch,

which feed on the caterpillars but never damage any vital part. The caterpillar lives on until ready to pupate, when it dies, and the grubs come through the skin and turn into tiny yellow cocoons. That is why the dead skin of a caterpillar is often found on a wall with a mass of these cocoons near it. They are sometimes called caterpillars' eggs, which is a misnomer, as only adult butterflies lay eggs. Do not destroy these cocoons : it is only this parasite which prevents epidemics every year.

8. Grease Bands Around Trees.—Put grease bands around the fruit tree stems to catch the wingless females of various moths which from now on ascend the trees to lay their eggs in the branches. The males are winged, but the females, not being able to fly, must climb. Grease bands are a good way of catching them.

9. Pick Fruit ; Root-Prune Trees.—Pick fruit as ready, not before. Windfalls should be picked up and put for immediate use. Root-pruning of vigorous fruit trees may begin.

10. Put Cloches over Lettuce and Endive growing outside ; Blanch Endive to keep up supply ; Begin Sowing Mustard and Cress inside at Fortnightly Intervals.

SEPTEMBER—5th WEEK

1. Lift and Store Chicory and Celeriac.—Lift roots of chicory and cut off the tops to within an inch of the root. Store in sand in a suitable place outside until wanted for forcing. Lift celeriac and store in the same way as turnips and other roots.

2. Prepare Pea-Seed ; Harvest Haricots.—Peas grown for seed and hung in a sunny position or a shed to finish off should be shelled as soon as possible. Put the seeds in flat trays and put them in a sunny window to dry completely. Stir them occasionally. Haricot beans sown late and only now ripening should be harvested and hung to dry in an airy place.

◀ **Mr. MIDDLETON** says : *Fertilizers must be studied, and used in*

3. Begin the Big Clean Up.—The cleaning up of the garden should now begin. All *rottable* refuse must be put on the compost heap, and all coarse, wooden or diseased material put for burning. Hedges should be clipped and the trimmings put for the bonfire. Choose a good day for this, and get the burning done early so that there is no danger of breaking the black-out rules. If the fire is burning late in the day, cover with soil. Even one that has apparently finished may blaze up if a wind rises. Do not water bonfire ashes to put them out, as this only wastes valuable fertilizer. Later, pick out the charcoal and unburnt pieces, and store the ash for use in potting soils or on the onion bed.

4. Bring in Tomatoes.—Any tomato plants still outside should be cut and brought inside to finish. The whole plant can be hung up and the fruit removed as it ripens, or the trusses can be cut and hung over wires, or the fruit may be picked and put in boxes of cotton-wool or straw to ripen. Outdoor fruits are often mis-shapen or cracked, but they are good for cooking. Plants in pots should have been in earlier.

5. Maintain Salads.—Maintain the production of salads by supplies from outside, from cloches or frames. Do not expect later lettuce to heart quite so fully as summer ones. They are quite good without hearts. Any cos lettuce which are nearly fully grown should be tied around the middle to blanch the centre leaves a little.

6. Lift Radish ; Feed Broccoli.— The large radish, such as *Black Spanish* and *China Rose*, should be ready for lifting. Store in sand like carrots or beet. Feed broccoli, which will mature before Christmas. A light dressing of general fertilizer should be adequate.

7. Finish Outdoor Peas.—Outdoor peas will now be coming to an end. Use and remove the haulms. Cut the tops and leave the roots in the soil so that the bacteria in the nodules on the roots remain there.

8. Harvest Swedes.—Swedes can now be harvested. They would stand outside for some weeks yet, but it is wiser to get them into store and the land cleared for digging.

9. Prepare Leeks for Seed.—Where leeks have been grown for seed, the flower heads may still be green. If so, cut them with a long stalk and stand in water in a greenhouse. Those that are a little more advanced may be cut with a long stem, tied in small bundle, and hung in the greenhouse to ripen. A sheet of paper can be spread beneath the bundles to catch any seed that may fall later. Keep the atmosphere of the house dry. Seed saved from good plants, if well ripened, usually gives good results. Never save seed from current year's plants which have bolted.

10. Harvest Fruit ; Hoe.—Harvest fruits as ready and put in store-room or attic. Hoe between newly-planted strawberries where desirable.

11. Order Fruit.—When fruit is to be planted it is advisable to calculate the requirements and to order from a reliable nurseryman without delay. Specify November delivery, but do not be too exacting. The nurseryman may have to use his discretion and delay lifting the plants if the weather has been dry for a considerable time. Find out the reason for any delay.

12. Put in Cuttings.—Put in hard-wood cuttings of currant and goose-berries. Cut them 10-in. long from current year's wood. All the buds are left on blackcurrants, but only the top three or four on red currants and goose-berries. The lower ones, which would be underground, should be removed. Insert in the open garden 9-in. apart.

13. Prune Fruit. — Prune Morello cherries now. Prune loganberries and blackberries, if not already done, by cutting out the growths which have fruited this year. Tie in the young shoots.

proper proportions, to ensure a balanced diet for the crops. ▶

OCTOBER—1st WEEK

1. Store Pea Sticks.—Pea sticks are hard to get, so those used this year should be cleaned and stored for use next year. Put under a shed, if available, or in a dry corner. Sticks which are rotting should be burnt with the other garden rubbish.

2. Get Stocks of Lime and Fertilizer.—Now is the time to calculate your lime and fertilizer requirements. Make an application of lime at least once in three years at the rate of ½-pound to the square yard. On acid soils, or those infected with clubroot, give heavier dressings and more often. A good general fertilizer, such as the National Growmore Fertilizer, containing the essential foods, will meet most requirements. Allow for a dressing all over the plot, at least 1 pound to 10 square yards, before sowing or planting, and another light application to growing plants. A total of 45 pounds should be enough for a standard allotment of 300 square yards.

3. Lift Root Crops.—Jerusalem artichokes may now be cut down to within a foot of the soil. They can be lifted and stored if the land is wanted for digging, but otherwise may be left outside, since they are quite hardy. Any carrots, beet, turnips, kohl rabi, celeriac or other plants remaining outside should be lifted and stored. The last potatoes should be lifted as soon as possible and clamped. Cover with straw, but leave for a day or two to sweat before putting soil layer over.

4. Earth-up Winter Greens and Celery.—Winter greens can now be earthed-up. A little soil drawn around the stems gives added protection. Earth-up celery. Late cauliflowers should be cut as they mature, and the earliest broccoli will now be turning in.

5. Protect Endive.—Endive, growing outside, should be moved to a frame now, or cloches put over the rows. Frost and bad weather damage the leaves. Trap or poison slugs if they tend to live on the endive.

6. Good-bye to Tomatoes.—Tomatoes, indoors, when finished should be pulled up, the stem chopped, and placed on the compost heap. Do not wait until the very last fruit has ripened. The few green ones left can be made into chutney or ripened in a warm room. When grown on benches the soil should be removed and put outside. It should be discarded if fresh loam is available for next year, but if not, place in layers with farmyard manure between. This should remain unused for two years if possible.

7. Clean Out Greenhouse.—Clean out the greenhouse, moving pots, boxes and canes, and string from the wires. As soon as practicable wash down the greenhouse, scrubbing all the woodwork and cleaning the glass. Where mildew or a bad attack of red spider mite has been present, spray the greenhouse with formaldehyde or cresylic acid and leave closed for a day or two.

8. Look to Raspberries and Strawberries.—Raspberries newly planted last year should have produced growths from the base. Tie them in. Strawberries may still be planted.

◄ **Mr. MIDDLETON** says : *Celery is by nature a bog plant,*

9. Store Fruit.—Store good fruit in wrappers. If space is limited, store in boxes or clamp outside.

10. Cut Parsley for Drying ; Do Not Delay Grease-Banding Fruit Trees.

OCTOBER—2nd WEEK

1. Earth-up Leeks.—Leeks, like other winter greens, should be given a good earthing-up, even those grown in holes. This gives protection as well as blanching the stems.

2. Cut Down and Weed Asparagus.— The foliage of asparagus will now be brown or yellow. Cut it down to the ground and put for burning. During the summer a thick growth of weeds, particularly grass, will have sprung up, and will need cleaning out. Tidy up the bed and put on a layer of farmyard manure, topped with a little soil.

3. Begin Digging.—In the rest of the garden where it is clear of crops, a beginning should be made on digging. Do not wait until all the garden is cleared, as some will be occupied until spring. The sooner digging is begun the better, even though only a small piece is dug at a time. This applies to ordinary, not sandy, soils.

4. Attend to Cabbage, Sprouts, Cauliflowers.—Run the Dutch hoe between spring cabbage for the last time, drawing a little soil up to the stems. Where they are planted in drills leave alone. In the south plantings may still be made, but in colder parts it is better to finish planting early in October. Cabbages will be keeping up a steady supply of greens, and the earliest Savoys will be ready. Brussels sprouts may also be ready, but it is still a little early to get the best value from them. These button up much better in a firm soil, so firm them with the feet where they are at all loose. Remove the leaves from the bottom as they turn yellow. Seedling cauliflowers from September sowings can be pricked out into a frame.

5. Plant Lettuce in Greenhouse.—In the greenhouse, when the tomatoes are cleared, plant lettuce. Where the house has been washed down, leave for a week or so to dry. Turn over the soil to assist this. Make successional sowing of mustard and cress.

6. Transplant Fruit.—Suckers from raspberries may be dug up and transplanted to increase the number of plants. Move only clean and healthy ones. Avoid any showing signs of virus disease, or those with mottled or wrinkled foliage. A beginning can also be made on transplanting fruit bushes if this is necessary. Young currants and gooseberries put in as cuttings a year ago can now be moved.

7. Store Apples.—Pick fruits on dry days as ready. A large quantity of apples needs a lot of housing, and cooking varieties can be clamped like potatoes. Smaller quantities are better wrapped with paper and placed in deep boxes. Dig a hole in the garden, line it with straw, and put the box of apples inside. Cover with straw and soil until wanted. Allow late-keeping apples to remain on trees as long as possible.

8. Grease-Banding Tips.—Complete grease-banding as soon as possible. Tie 6–9-in. strips of greaseproof paper around the stems of the trees and smear all round some good sticky material. Special greases are available for this work. A good grease is not washed off by the rain nor melted by the sun.

9. Lift and Store Salsify and Scorzonera ; Store Unused Garlic ; Sort and Clean Shallots.

10. Encourage Fruit Trees. Old and backward trees can often be helped by scraping away two or three inches of soil and replacing with new. Prune away dead branches from tree.

OCTOBER—3rd WEEK

1. Order of Using Vegetables.—There will still be ample supplies of food from the open garden as well as from store. Use such things as cabbages, cauliflowers, and early Savoys, before going on to the hardier vegetables, such as

and requires abundance of water. Never allow it to get dry. ▶

leeks, which should be left until other foods become scarcer. Of course the time of maturing is governed by the season, and in some years crops will turn-in much earlier than in others. Premature sowing and planting also cause this, which is why a record should be kept of all crops for future guidance. The correct times for your own garden can only be learned by experience. Most of the winter crops are improved in flavour if they have been touched by frost.

2. Prepare Potting Composts.—No opportunity should be lost of acquiring soil and other ingredients of potting composts. For such work, ordinary soil dug from the garden is not the best, particularly if it has been cultivated for some years or is surrounded by trees and bushes. The best loam is obtained by stacking turves and leaving for 12 months before using. These are not so easy to come by nowadays, but you may be lucky. Other soil should be stacked in layers with manure in between.

3. Clean Outside Greenhouse.—The outside of greenhouses should be washed as well as the inside. Where shading has been applied, such as whitewash or *Summer Cloud*, to protect tomatoes or cucumbers from strong sunlight, this should be scrubbed off. The most must be made of daylight during the winter. Frame lights, too, should be cleaned of grime.

4. Make Fruit Plan.—If you are to plant fruit for the first time, plan your garden just as you would for vegetables. Arrange the position of everything. Order what you want without delay, and choose varieties of tree fruits which are likely to succeed. Remember that many varieties are self-sterile and need to be mixed so that they will fertilize each other. If you plant only one variety you may get no fruit, even though they flower abundantly.

5. How to Destroy Red Spider.—Where red spider mite has been bad on wall fruit, such as peaches and nectarines, the leaves should be collected and burned. At this time of the year the small pests move to cracks and crannies in walls and woodwork to hibernate. It is a good tip to put straw down on the floor in August. Many of them will enter the straw for the winter, when the straw can be swept up and burned. Painting the inside woodwork kills many and seals the cracks.

COMPOST HEAP FORMATION (see also page **17**)

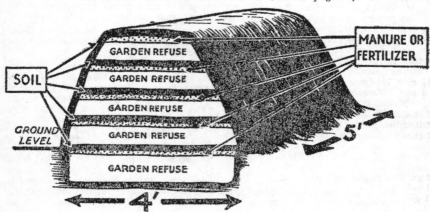

◀ Mr. MIDDLETON says: *Don't spray fruit trees on a windy*

6. Protect Carrots.—Carrots in frames should be protected now with glass.

7. Earth-up Celery.—Give final earthing-up to celery. Smooth the sides of the ridge with spade.

8. Take Dead Leaves from Rhubarb ; Plant Late Coleworts in South ; Prune and Tie-in Blackberries.

OCTOBER—4th WEEK

1. Retard and Force Rhubarb.—Lift a root of rhubarb and leave it exposed to the weather for a fortnight. The harder the season the better, as the action of frost is to produce a certain amount of sugar in the root and this is readily available for the sticks when they begin to grow. This is known as retarding. To obtain sticks at Christmas from the open garden, forcing should begin now.

2. Nurse Parsley.—Parsley growing out of doors will come through the winter quite successfully if it is a mild one, but it is better to take precautions. Put some timber around the patch and cover with a frame light. When making the late sowing in July it is wise to allow for this and sow a piece about the size of a light.

3. Plant Fruit Trees.—The fruit trees and bushes you have ordered may arrive any time. As soon as they do, dig a trench, put in the roots, cover with soil and tread it down. This is known as heeling in, and it is most important not to leave the roots at all exposed. They will be quite safe like this until you are ready to plant them. See that plants, old and new, are labelled.

4. Manuring.—Calculate your future requirements of manure. Order hop manure if other natural manures are not available. Get spent hops and sewage sludge if you can. Dig-in green manure.

5. Sow and Plant.—Sow round-seeded spinach in cold frame. Plant lettuce in cold frame or greenhouse, and water carefully. Lettuce outside should be protected with cloches.

6. Prune Fruit.—Begin pruning fruit as soon as leaves have fallen.

7. Ventilate Cauliflowers in Frames ; Examine Fruit in Store.

ONE YEAR'S SUPPLIES FOR YOUR GARDEN

Here is a table of quantities of various recommended materials, sufficient for a year's needs in a garden of 300 square yards.

For Open Garden Cultivation

1 ton Farmyard Manure, or compost-heap refuse.
1½ cwt. Hydrated Lime.
½ cwt. General Fertilizer, such as National Growmore Fertilizer.
7 lbs. Dried Blood.
7 lbs. Bone Meal.
7 lbs. Sulphate of Ammonia.

For Pest and Disease Control

1/2 lbs. Calomel Dust.
7 lbs. Crude Naphthalene.
3 lbs. Flowers of Sulphur.
4 fluid ounces Nicotine (98 per cent.).
4 lbs. Derris Dust, *or*
4 lbs. Proprietary Derris.

For Fruit Garden

2 gallons Tar-Distillate, *or*
2 gallons Petroleum Wash, *or*
1 gallon Lime Sulphur.

2 gallons D.N.C. (Dinitro-ortho-cresol).
1 large tin Grease, such as Tangle-foot.

day. Tar oil is no good to green vegetables, or to washing next door. ▶

NOVEMBER—*1st* WEEK

1. Secure Clamps.—All clamps should be made firm and secure now for the winter. Soil should be banked around them, where not thick enough, and patted down. In siting clamps in the ordinary garden a position easily accessible from the house is desirable, so that when they are opened it is easy for the housewife to get what is required. The position should be well drained, too, though the trenches made when excavating the soil help considerably in this respect.

2. Carry On Digging.—Carry on digging as convenient. Apart from the beneficial effect on the soil of early digging, it is wise to complete as much as possible while the weather remains open. The really bad weather usually comes after Christmas, and if your digging is not done by then you may be held up until spring. The first portion to be dug should be the onion bed. A firm, deeply dug soil is necessary for these, so double-dig now, breaking up the subsoil, and incorporate such manure as you can get. This will give time for the soil to settle. Ridge the soil if it is heavy, and so expose a greater surface to the action of the weather (see *Ridging*). If you have the time—and the energy—the onion bed should be bastard trenched. This breaks it up more deeply still, which is all to the good (see *Bastard Trenching*).

3. Care of Soil in Frames.—The soil in frames around the salad crops and seedlings sets on top, and often a green crust (called *algae*) grows there. It pays to break this, and the soil should be stirred with a pointed stick, or where space allows with a small hand-fork. Air the frames daily, pushing the lights off completely on good days, and pulling them on again in the evening. Water carefully and only when really necessary. Do not let water get on the leaves of lettuce, as it causes decay. Slugs are a great nuisance in frames during winter. Always keep your eyes open for them.

4. Sow Peas.—In the south and midlands choose a sheltered spot and sow a row of a round-seeded pea, such as *Blue Bird*. Peas will be obtained a month earlier than with post-Christmas sowings. Such a sowing is not worth while in the north, where losses are too heavy during the winter, and any that do come through rarely gain on later sowings.

5. Sow Broad Beans and Onions.—Broad beans, too, should be sown on a warm border. Put the seed in drills 12-in. wide, 2-in. deep and 2-ft. apart. Space them out 9 in. each way, as a double row. This sowing also gains little in the north, though the plants will grow quite successfully. Autumn-sown onions are normally fairly successful outside, but in places where it is doubtful if they will survive the winter, give some protection. Either cover with cloches or a temporary frame.

6. Free Tree Branches.—Standard fruit trees, apples, pears, plums and cherries are not normally pruned except for the removal of dead branches. Should any be crowded, or if two cross each other, then remove one. Congestion of the branches spoils the trees. Clear up around trees.

◀ Mr. MIDDLETON says : *Plum trees do not like the knife, which*

NOVEMBER—4th WEEK

1. Lift and Store Swede Turnips.—
Swede turnips can remain out of doors
a long time without hardship, but there
is no point in letting them do so. Lift
them, cut off the tops, and store in a
clamp in the same way as potatoes. A
small quantity can be kept in sacks.
All tops and other leaves from the garden, such as those of Brussels sprouts,
should be used to finish off the summer
compost heap. Mound it up with soil
and leave for a few months to decay.
Begin a new heap to take winter rubbish
from the house and garden.

2. Clear Artichokes.—Lift and use
Jerusalem artichokes and make sure
the land is clear of them. Pick out a
few tubers for replanting purposes.
Examine crops in store at regular
intervals.

3. Examine Clamps.—After heavy
rains the sides of clamp sometimes need
banking up, and a watch should be kept
for signs of rats. They may find their
way into a clamp and do a lot of damage.
As soon as first signs are seen put some
poison down.

4. Examine Onions and Shallots.—
Onions stored inside, if well ripened, will
be quite good for a long time yet.
Grown in a rainy season, they may not
be as firm as is desirable and their
keeping qualities are not of the best.
Any showing signs of softening should
be used early, while decayed specimens
should be burned. Shallots being kept
for replanting should be turned over
occasionally. Double the quantity required should always be stored to allow
for losses.

5. Clear Mushrooms.— Mushroom
beds which are finished should be cleaned
out and replaced with new ones. The
manure is ideal for use in soil mixtures,
or for digging into frames and such like
places where fresh manure is not
desirable.

6. Pick Kales.—Pickings from kales
can now be used. In some parts
growth takes place most of the winter,

*Reward
of
good
gardening*

but in others bad weather causes the
large leaves to die and drop off. The
plants often look rather poor and
miserable in January, but by March
growth has begun again, and from then
until June there is a steady supply of
greens.

7. Examine Grease Bands.—Greasebands should be examined regularly.
Dead leaves and small twigs which
adhere to them must be removed, as
these provide a bridge over which the
moths can crawl. By the way, it is
important that stakes should also have
a band around them, otherwise the
insects will by-pass those on the tree
and reach the branches.

8. Raise Carrots.—Young carrots can
be raised in a deep frame if hot-bed
material is not available.

**9. Complete Summer Compost Heap
and Begin New One.**

garden, but by deep digging you can make more soil available for crops. ▶

DECEMBER—1st WEEK

1. Maintain Successions of Rhubarb and Chicory.—Maintain successions of the crops which are forced, such as chicory and rhubarb. Lift a crown of rhubarb each fortnight and leave exposed to the weather. Do not pick odd ones here and there in the plantation, but start at the end of a row and work along it systematically. The cleared piece can then be dug, manured and replanted in spring. Forced roots should either be destroyed or replanted, and left for two years or so, without cutting, to recover. Cover a clump out of doors to provide supplies after Christmas. Where no greenhouse is available for forcing a warm shed can be used, or a deep cold frame in which a hot-bed can be made. Put in a deep layer of fresh manure, firm it down, and force the roots over it.

2. Prepare for Bad Weather.—It is a good plan to get ready materials such as hessian or sacks for covering frames if bad weather sets in. The gardener is always weather-conscious, and never more so than in winter. Frosts must always be anticipated, and you soon get the knack. Additional protection will be necessary during prolonged hard weather, and some straw should be obtained for this.

3. Clear Cucumber.—The remains of cucumbers can be removed. Wash and clean the house after them, and if pests have been troublesome, spray it inside thoroughly with formaldehyde or cresylic acid. If grown on a border, the soil

can be dug and planted with lettuce; but should they be on a bench, the soil can be carted outside or smoothed down, and a sowing of mustard and cress made on it. In foggy weather a thick layer of soot and dirt is deposited on the glass of greenhouses and frames. It should be washed off before it sets hard as soon as the weather clears.

4. Review Your Gardening Year.—Now is the time to complete the notes of operations in the garden and the various successes and failures. For example, if you think it will be better to sow a certain crop a fortnight later than you did, because it matured too soon this year, make a note of it to make sure you do not forget.

5. Make Use of Frosty Days.—During frosty weather, when the ground is hard, take the opportunity to wheel materials across or on to the garden. For instance, if you are going to put farmyard manure around your trees and bushes, wheel it now and tip in heaps. It saves a lot of carrying.

6. Finish Pruning.—Try to complete all pruning by January, so that the way will be clear for spraying. There is no point in spraying wood which will be cut away. Rake up the prunings and burn them. Newly-planted trees which have not been pruned by the nurseryman should be left until spring before cutting them. The reason is to avoid a double check of severed roots and cut branches. By spring the roots will be growing and the trees able to stand pruning. Like most things in gardening, there are two schools of thought on this

◀ Mr. MIDDLETON says : *A swede forced in the dark after*

subject, but the course suggested is the safer.

7. **Dig.**—Do your best to get digging done before Christmas. Clean between bushes, and give a shallow forking. Buy stocks of spraying materials.

DECEMBER—2nd WEEK

1. **Draw Up Plans.**—Draw up your plans now or during Christmas week if you have a little spare time. Use your old plans as a basis and have your notes beside you to freshen your memory about alterations you intended to make. Calculate your seed requirements and write out your seed order and send it off. Look over your seed potatoes.

2. **Keep Digging.**—Dig, too, when you can, even though it is only a little at a time. Either ridge or leave the surface rough. That does not mean leave ground in humps and hollows, looking rather like a battlefield. What is meant is that the soil is kept level, but the spadefuls are just turned over and left without being chopped up.

3. **Gather Greens.**—The supply of greens from the garden should be steadily maintained. There is a wide choice, cabbage—*Christmas Drumhead* in particular—Savoys, Brussels sprouts, broccoli, kales, perpetual spinach and leeks. In some parts lettuce may be available from the open garden or from cloches, as well as endive.

4. **Preserve Labels.**—Good garden labels, particularly the larger ones, are valuable, and as many as possible should be saved. Do not leave them lying about outside. A job for wet week-ends is to scrape them and then repaint them ready for use. They can be scraped fairly clean by using the edge of a piece of glass.

5. **Grow Mint and Chives Indoors.**—Put a few roots of mint in a box and bring into a greenhouse or warm room for forcing. Chives, too, can be grown inside. Pot up a few roots and they will give a succession of soft green shoots during winter for flavouring.

6. **Look to Spring Cabbage.**—A few of the first-planted spring cabbage may begin to heart up if the weather remains open and mild. They will only spoil, and should be cut for use. Draw soil up to the others where necessary.

7. **Remove Fruit-Tree Suckers.**—In going through the fruit trees, suckers which have grown up from the roots during the summer should be cut out. Do not cut down to the surface, but follow them beneath the soil and sever as low as possible.

8. **Plant Cob-Nuts and Fruit Trees.**—Anyone with a good large garden should plant a few cob-nut trees. They could be made to form part of an ordinary shrubbery, or planted as a surround to the fruit garden. Thin out old nut trees, but leave real pruning until after flowering. You can still plant fruit trees if weather is open.

9. **Sow Tomatoes.**—Tomatoes may be sown for spring crop in greenhouse.

DECEMBER—3rd WEEK

1. **Collect Leaves.**—Take every opportunity from October onwards to collect tree leaves. They generally collect in drifts and are easy to pick up. Small quantities can be added to the compost heap, but where more are available make special heaps. Some can be used for forcing purposes, as thick layers of them soon heap up. Decayed leaves, as a source of humus for the soil, are of great value.

2. **Attend to Broad Beans and Peas.**—Broad beans growing out of doors from the November sowing will be a few inches high. Normally they will be quite happy without protection, but it will help if a little soil is drawn up to the sides of the rows. In more doubtful cases a few twigs pushed in alongside the rows will give good cover. Peas will also be through and will need protection from birds. Put wire covers over, or thread black cotton over the rows to scare them off. Stakes pushed in now will give protection as well as support.

3. **Clean Paths.**—Paths should be scraped as the land is dug, skimming off any weeds, such as grass, and throwing

Christmas produces white tops which you will find as good as seakale. ▶

them into the trenches, so that when the work is finished the whole presents a tidy appearance. When there is much walking about soil gets trodden on to the paths, and this must be scraped up before frost makes it hard. When frozen it is a nuisance both to walk on and to wheel barrows over. Pots and boxes lying about should be tidied up and re-arranged, not merely because they are precious, but because pests find them ideal to hibernate in, quite apart from rats and mice.

4. Cut Perpetual Spinach.—Perpetual spinach from summer sowings should be in regular use. Cut the large leaves from a number of plants, rather than cut one plant down to the base.

5. Look for Big Bud on Blackcurrants.—Blackcurrants suffering from big bud mite should get attention now. Moderate infection shows itself in only a small number of swollen buds. These will now be obvious and should be picked off and burned. Where a high proportion of the buds are infected it is better to grub up the bushes and burn them. Buy clean stock.

6. Look to Frames.—Ventilate crops growing in frames, especially spring cabbage in the north. Sow lettuce in boxes for planting in greenhouse after Christmas.

7. Order Seeds Now ; Overhaul Spraying Apparatus.

DECEMBER—4th WEEK

1. Christmas Jobs.—This being Christmas week will for some be a week of rest ; for others it will provide opportunities for some work in the garden, weather permitting. There is never any lack of jobs to do in the garden, and Christmas provides an opportunity for getting up to date with many of them, particularly for the busy man. Where there are frames and a greenhouse there is sure to be something to do irrespective of the weather.

2. Lift Celery.—Celery should now be in steady use. Lift each plant as you require it. In hard weather cover the rows with straw or bracken as a

protection and to keep them accessible. A few can be lifted and put in the corner of a frame, covered with soil to keep them white and crisp. As the crop is cleared from outside, level off the land and dig. The site will be ideal for parsnips or long-rooted carrots, as it was well manured for the celery. These crops fare better on land manured the previous year. Fresh manure should never be added for root crops, as it tends to induce coarseness and splitting of the roots. Both carrots and parsnips fork or produce fangs.

3. Erect Wind Breaks.—Dry, cold winds cutting along over the soil surface often do a tremendous amount of damage to plants. Against these, wind breaks should be erected to protect things like spring cabbage. Wattle hurdles are the best : pushed in along the windward sides of crops they save much damage. Failing hurdles, twigs and sticks are helpful. Twiggy branches laid over crops break the force of wind and frost.

4. Complete Fruit Planting.—Complete fruit planting as quickly as possible. The chief reason for planting in November is that the soil still retains some warmth, and so is helpful to a little initial root growth, but by now this advantage is almost gone. If planting is not done this week it will be better to wait until March, which is a little before the soil begins to warm again. Do not overcrowd any trees or bushes merely because they seem small. Allow for their ultimate size. The spaces in between can always be used for vegetables until the trees are larger.

5. Fruit Trees and Whitewash.—It is a common sight to see the bottom 3 or 4 ft. of the trunks of fruit trees whitewashed. Formerly this cleaned the main stems, but in these days of spraying with winter washes it is quite unnecessary.

6. Keep Supplies Going.—Maintain a supply of mustard and cress and radishes. Force seakale and chicory for regular use. Lift another root of rhubarb for inside forcing. Protect

◀ Mr. MIDDLETON says : *Stick a bit of holly in the pudding,*

corn salad. Pull up stumps of cut greens, and clean away dead leaves from others.

DECEMBER—5th WEEK

1. Clean Up and Dig.—This, the last week of the year, is a good time to complete such jobs as tidying up, cleaning paths, etc., and to finish the digging and trenching. Land dug now and left rough has a good three months in which to weather. When forked in spring the rough lumps fall easily, and a fine tilth is produced, much superior to that produced by digging late and forking through immediately afterwards. Apply quicklime to soil.

2. Order Seeds.—Draw the garden plan if not done, before the year is out, and send off for your seeds. Give trials to a new variety or two, different from those you grew last year. Should this be your first year, order the stock varieties of most vegetables, that is, those sold by all seedsmen as distinct from varieties bearing their own name. They are often printed in small type in the catalogues. Better still, contact a good local gardener or your horticultural adviser and find out the varieties which are usually grown in your district.

3. Prepare Greenhouse.—Prepare the greenhouse for seed-sowing and the slowly increasing amount of work. Wash it down if not done earlier. Tidy up boxes and pots, get soil, leaf mould, sand, peat and fertilizers ready. If possible, sterilize the soil first.

4. Anticipate Frost.—It may seem as though a fairly long period of frost is likely. This will bind the soil hard, and it will be found difficult to get up such crops as parsnips, leeks and celery. This should be anticipated, and while it is still possible a good quantity of these should be lifted and heeled together in the end of a frame. The parsnips can be stored in sand. When roots are wanted from outdoor clamps, remove the soil from one end and move the straw. Get out what is wanted, replace the straw and throw a good sack over.

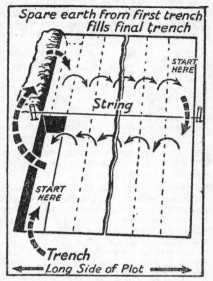

Dig your garden by dividing it down the middle and beginning with a trench across one half

This is easily lifted when further supplies are required. Onions in store may begin to produce green shoots. These should be put out for early use, for otherwise they will become soft.

5. Prune, and Prepare for Spraying Fruit.—In the fruit garden complete pruning and get ready for spraying. See that your sprayer works well. Remember, a coarse nozzle is used for winter spraying. Make sure you have enough spray material to do all you want.

6. Plant Cauliflowers ; Sow Beans.—Plant out cauliflowers in cold house between larger lettuce. Sow broad beans in boxes for later planting out.

7. Make Hot-Bed.—Make up hotbed for growing salads, young carrots, etc. Also make up compost heap.

8. Put Strawberries in Greenhouse.—If you have room, you can now put strawberries in pots in a cold greenhouse.

if you've got a pudding, and do something to cheer yourself up. ▶

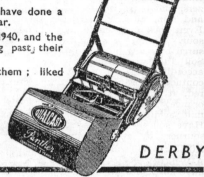

Middleton's Gardening Guide
ENCYCLOPAEDIA of GARDENING

A

ACID SOIL : Soils may be acid (i.e., sour), neutral, or alkaline. Most soils in this country are acid. Rain, continuous cultivation, addition of fertilizers, and extraction of lime by plants and rain, all tend to make them so. Even soils over chalk subsoil can be sour. Extent of acidity can be measured by using liquid known as B.D.H. Soil Indicator, which changes colour according to degree of acidity. If, upon contact with sample of soil, liquid turns red, it indicates extreme acidity ; if orange, moderate acidity ; if yellow, mild acidity ; if green, a neutral soil. Have soil tested occasionally : rectify sourness by applying lime.

ACRE : 4,840 square yards, or 160 rods.

ADVISORY SERVICES : Most towns have horticultural advisers—superintendent of parks—who will gladly help anyone in difficulties. Many large towns have appointed special advisers to help with Dig for Victory Campaign. In rural areas advisers are attached to County Education Authority and County War Agricultural Executive Committee.

ALGÆ : Class of lowly, non-flowering plants. They have no true stems or leaves, but contain chlorophyll, and are green. All parts of plant absorb food and moisture. Green slime on flower pots, on unstirred soil, sides of water tanks, on tree trunks, consists of algæ.

ALLIUM : (See *Onion.*) Botanical name for the onion group. Usually used only for decorative flowering forms.

ALLOTMENT : Well-cultivated plot of 300 square yards should keep family of four in vegetables whole year round.

ALPINE STRAWBERRY : Small strawberry which bears fruits from June onwards. Suitable for rock garden.

AMERICAN BLIGHT : (See *Woolly Aphis.*)

AMERICAN GOOSEBERRY MILDEW : White mildew seen in spring on shoots and young berries. Later turns brown. Common in Ireland, and has been epidemic in Great Britain. Usually appears May, starting on undersides of young leaves, and passes to berries and ruins them. Control measures : prune and burn infected shoots in winter ; spray in April with lime-sulphur at 1 in 30, as soon as flowers have set—half-strength for gooseberries which cannot stand full strength. Yellow gooseberries should be sprayed with ammonium polysulphide, which can be bought as proprietary article. Where more than one spraying needed, it should always be substituted for lime-sulphur. Flowers of sulphur or washing soda can also be used.

AMMONIA : Ordinary household ammonia can be applied to soil as insecticide. Dilute ½ pint with 1 gallon of water and pour on 2–3 square yards of soil. Cover with sacks for few days to gives fumes chance to kill any pests. Do not confuse with sulphate of ammonia (which see).

ANBURY : Clubroot disease of brassicas.

ANGELICA : Herb whose roots and leaves have medicinal properties. Stems are candied and used in confectionery, and oil is distilled from roots and seeds. Raised from seed and reaches 6 ft. in height.

ANNUAL : Plant which germinates from seed, reaches maturity, flowers, and produces seed itself in one year. Annuals can only be raised from seeds. Some vegetables are annuals, e.g., lettuce, though most are biennials.

ANTS : Troublesome in garden, particularly among young seedlings in greenhouse. They eat fruit but normally are not initial cause of damage. When fruits have been attacked by birds or

◀ Mr. MIDDLETON says : *The soil produces everything we possess.* ▶

wasps they will follow. Strawberries are exception, and ants will directly attack ripe fruits. Worst fault is that they carry about aphids (greenfly). Aphids feed on the sap of plants until it overflows. Ants like this surplus sap, called *honey dew*, and treat aphids as cows, milking them by massaging with their antennæ. Destroy ants' nests with boiling water, nicotine, or strong disinfectant. Where nests cannot be found, poisoned syrup is best control. Dissolve 6 ozs. of sugar in 1 pint hot water and add 10 grains sodium arsenite. Place in tin lids, or soak in sponge and put this in perforated tin.

ANTHER : Male parts of flower, carrying pollen.

APHIS : (Plural *Aphids*.) Known as greenfly, plant bugs, plant lice, or "blight." Soft-bodied, sucking insects feeding on sap of plants and trees. Most plants have species of aphis parasite. They are small creatures, of various colours and often have markings on back. Have a special beak or proboscis to push through skin of leaf into cells. Breed speedily and set up large colonies in short time. First come in spring from eggs laid previous autumn, and at once produce living young, which quickly produce more young. Cause serious damage. To control, use spray to suffocate or poison them. A wash of nicotine and soft soap does both when directed at creatures to cover them. Poisoning food, as for biting insects like caterpillars, is no use against those that suck food. Winter spraying of fruit trees destroys eggs of species which attack fruit.

APPLE : Smaller trained types of apple trees, such as bush, cordon, and espalier trees, are best for average garden. Standard and half-standard are usually too large. Get expert advice on varieties suited to district.

APPLE BLOSSOM WEEVIL : Unopened flower buds of apple are attacked by this. Female lays eggs in bud, and larva feeds inside and destroys it. Attacked blossoms are said to be

Aphis on Blackcurrant

"capped" and should be collected and burned. Sack-bands can be fastened round trunks of trees in May and left until November. Adult weevils will hibernate in sacks and can be destroyed. Winter spraying with tar-distillate washes destroys a few.

APPLE MILDEW : White, powdery mildew which attacks tips of apple shoots and may attack flower blossoms. Best control is to cut out mildewed shoots in spring. This is not possible with larger bushes. Spray for apple scab helps.

APPLE SAWFLY : Female lays eggs singly in flowers of apple just below calyx. Eggs hatch after ten days. Young larvæ find way to small fruitlet and bore way in at side, eating out large cavities. Later, attacked fruits fall to ground and should be burned. Poultry under the trees will destroy large number. Best control is to spray with nicotine after eggs have hatched and while young larvæ are still exposed.

APPLE SUCKER : Larvæ attack young leaves, flowers and buds of apple trees. Eggs are laid in bark of trees in autumn

◀ **Mr. MIDDLETON** says : *Somebody told me recently*

and early winter. Control by winter spraying. Ordinary tar-distillate wash is very good, as eggs are completely exposed. Petroleum wash, such as winter Volck, is added to improve control. D.N.C. spray is said to be good control.

ARSENATE OF LEAD : Poison frequently applied to plants as spray to kill biting insects such as caterpillars. Mix with water at the rate of half a lb. to ten gallons of water, and apply as fine spray so as to give good cover to foliage. Unsuitable for plants, such as cabbages, likely to be eaten soon. Derris is equally effective and non-poisonous to humans. On fruit trees lead arsenate is efficient and safe if applied after blossom time. It should never be used while bees are active on trees.

ARTICHOKE : There are three kinds of so-called artichokes, the *Jerusalem*, the *Chinese*, and the *Globe* or true artichoke. Jerusalem is of chief interest to ordinary gardener. It is tall-growing perennial, really a variety of sunflower, having a tuberous root. Suitable tubers, about the size of egg, are picked out for planting as early in year as possible, preferably in February. Any rough corner can be used for them, or can be grown as hedge or windbreak to vegetable plot. Do not plant where they will overshadow other crops. One row is enough for average household. Take out drill 4- or 5-in. deep, and space out tubers 12-in. apart. Cover with soil. When tops are yellowing in autumn, cut down to within a foot of ground. Lift tubers for use as required. Do not leave any in soil to run wild. *White Jerusalem* is favourable variety. Where more than one row is planted allow 3 ft. between them.

ASHES : Ashes from household fires should never be put on garden except in heaviest clay soils, which they help to break up and make lighter. Wood ashes are beneficial. They contain potash, now one of scarcest of plant foods, and should always be saved. After a bonfire collect ashes together and protect from rain. Rain removes the potash. Use for dressing onion bed, and where peas and beans are to grow.

ASPARAGUS : Delightful vegetable which should be grown only where plenty of room and after all other vegetable requirements have been met. It is permanent crop and occupies same land for twenty years or more. Buy three-year-old male crowns, or raise from seeds. Plant in beds 4½-5 ft. wide, during April, three rows 18 in. apart, with 15 in. from crown to crown. Cover with soil, digging out path 2-ft. wide all round and building up bed 6-in. high. Begin to cut following year. Never cut after mid-June, but allow growths to develop. Cut down stems in late autumn, clean beds, mulch with manure and with top soil. Build up beds again before growth begins in spring.

AXIL : Name given to hollow where base of leaf joins stem. Normal place for growth buds and side shoots to be produced.

B

BARK RINGING : Simple method of checking growth of over-vigorous fruit trees which produce poor crops. Usually done in May. There are two methods : (1) a complete ring of bark about ⅛-in. wide down to the hard wood is cut around trunk of the tree ; (2) two half-rings, one above other on opposite sides of tree, and about 4-in. apart. These rings are ½-in. wide, and upper half-ring should end immediately above lower. Cuts must be covered with adhesive tape or painted with white lead paint. Normally only apple and pear trees are so treated.

BASIC SLAG : Industrial by-product when iron is converted into steel. Molten iron is treated to remove impurities, and these float to surface as scum, which is poured off and sets in large cinders. To be useful in garden cinders are ground to very fine powder. Rich in lime and phosphorus and therefore useful fertilizer. Amount of phosphorus varies in different samples, but percentage, between 15 and 40 per cent., usually stated when slag is marketed.

that I had sprouting broccoli on the brain. Perhaps I have. ▶

Usually applied to land about ½-lb. per square yard, in November, to give time for foods to be released and made available to plants. Lime in it makes it useful on heavy land, and it is valuable where peas, beans, potatoes and roots, etc., are to be grown. Apply in fruit garden at approximately 2 lbs. per bush and 5 lbs. per tree.

BASTARD TRENCHING : (See *Double Digging*.) Method of ·digging whereby soil is dug two or three spits deep, as against one spit (10 in.) in ordinary single digging, and different layers are kept in their respective positions. In trenching proper (see *Trenching*), soil is dug two spits deep, but top soil is buried and subsoil brought to surface. Trenching should be attempted only when good soil has been buried. In Bastard or Mock Trenching, soil is cut out in steps (see illustration) and turned over a step at a time so that top soil remains at top. In good gardens one-third of area is done each year, thus digging whole deeply in three years. Amateurs rarely find time to do this, but should certainly do some double-digging each year. It is necessary where vegetables are grown for exhibition, and is worth while before planting fruit. Bastard trenching is sometimes done three-spits deep for special purposes, but is not practicable for ordinary gardener.

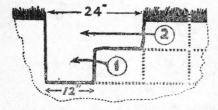

BASTARD TRENCHING : Move earth in square (1) across, and then move earth in square (2) on top of it

BEAN, BROAD : Hardy bean which likes well-dug strong soil. Seeds usually sown during winter, so that early crop shall not clash with peas. Chief types are dwarf *Early Magazan, Windsor* and *Longpod*. In south and midlands, sow first in November in sheltered position, and later for succession. In north the risks of early sowings are too great, and later-sown crops nearly always catch up first and pass them. Sow, then, as soon as weather and soil conditions permit. February is usually earliest month. Sow in drills 12-in. wide and 2–3-in. deep. Space out seeds 9-in. apart in double row. Cover with soil. Allow 2–2½-ft. between rows. Or sow in single rows 1½–2-ft. apart. Chief pest— *Black Fly* or *Bean Aphis* (for which see p. 81.)

BEAN, FRENCH or DWARF KIDNEY : Non-hardy beans which like rich, well-prepared soil. In south, seeds can be sown from mid-April onwards ; in north, May is soon enough. Sow in rows 9-in. between the seeds with rows 18-in. apart. Seeds may be put in twice as thick and thinned out to this distance, as insurance against failure of some. In cold weather and difficult districts plants can be raised in frames for planting out when conditions improve. Care is necessary when planting to avoid check to plants. Two sowings a month apart are normally sufficient for ordinary family. For larger supplies sow at fortnightly intervals until end of June.

BEAN, HARICOT : Similar to above, but grown for dried beans not green pods. Cultivate in same way as French beans, but leave pods on plants until they turn brown. Pull up plants, tie in bundles, and hang in airy shed until seeds can be shelled. Green pods can be eaten, and care should be taken when pulling dwarf beans not to take any of haricot-bean pods.
Varieties : *Comtesse de Chambord, Brown Dutch, Swiss White.*

BEAN, RUNNER : Scarlet-runner bean, ornamental as well as useful. Succeeds best in sheltered garden or grown up wall. Where shelter is difficult, keep pinched and grow as bush instead of up stakes. Choose site early, dig 12–18-in. deep trench in March, and leave open for

◀ Mr. MIDDLETON says : *If you want a good mallet, cut out a*

Two methods of supporting runner beans. Be sure that they are strong enough to stand up to a heavy crop, and wind.

STAKES   STRING

some weeks. Fork up subsoil. Before sowing put in good layer of farmyard manure or compost material, and fill to within 3 in. of level with soil. This forms a drill 12-in. wide. Put in the seeds, 12-in. apart in two rows, staggered. Cover with soil but do not quite fill trench. It is not safe to sow before May, towards the end of May in north. If more than one row is being grown, keep at least 6-ft. apart. Stake thoroughly, using whichever method suits you (see illustration). Hoe around the rows when necessary, water if required, damp the foliage and flowers occasionally, in dry areas mulch around the plants with leaves or manure.

Varieties : *Scarlet Emperor, Prizewinner, Streamline.*

BEAN APHIS or BLACK FLY : Regular pest of broad beans, which also attacks many other plants. Over-winters as egg on shrubs, such as elderberry or euonymus (spindle tree), from which in spring hatches female aphis, which gives birth to living young instead of laying eggs, and soon produces large colony. Females have wings and fly to other plants, preferably beans. Prevalent everywhere, but easy to control. It is soft-bodied, sucking insect which feeds on plant sap. If broad beans are pinched—i.e., soft tips of plant are removed when bottom whorl of flowers has set and are showing small

pods—attacks will be discouraged. Earlier sowings are less subject to attack than later. If infestation occurs, spray with good proprietary insecticide or nicotine spray. Insects must be hit and covered by spray, which must be aimed directly at them.

BEETROOT : Two chief kinds, the globe and the long-rooted. Former, more useful in home, as can be boiled in ordinary saucepan. Long-rooted type is sown in May as maincrop for storage, the drills being 18-in. apart and seeds put in thinly. Thin to 9 in. from plant to plant. The globe can be sown from March onwards in the south, April in north. Sow in drills 12-in. apart and thin to 6 in. Beet is maritime crop, and light dressing of salt can be applied to it while small.

Varieties : (*Long*) *Cheltenham Green Top, Blood Red* ; (*Globe*) *Empire Globe, Crimson Globe.*

BEET AND MANGOLD FLY : Female lays eggs inside leaf of beet, and grubs feed between upper and lower skins. Type of pest known as leaf-miner. Where attacks have been experienced, hoe naphthalene between rows to keep fly away. If leaves are attacked, spray forcibly with nicotine. Grubs can also be destroyed by squeezing them in leaf, but this is tedious job. Dig soil early in winter to expose pupæ to birds and frost.

piece of apple wood of the right size, and put an ash stick in it. ▶

BIENNIAL : Plant which requires two seasons to mature, that is, from sowing of seed to producing seeds. Many vegetables are biennials and are used during first season, e.g., carrot, onion, parsnip, all of which build up food storage organs the first year, and second year flower and produce seeds. Sowing seeds at wrong time, or some check to growth, will often make plants run to seed, or bolt as it is called.

Spray for big bud mite when blackcurrant leaves are the size of a shilling

BIG BUD MITE OF BLACKCURRANTS : Minute pest which lives during winter within tissues of blackcurrant buds, making them swell. Those attacked produce only malformed leaves. In spring, when buds begin to burst, mites leave their winter home and feed on outside of bushes. At this time they are most vulnerable. To control, spray bushes with lime-sulphur 1 in 13 on varieties which will stand it, such as *Baldwin*, but at 1 in 20 on varieties such as *Davison's Eight*, which tends to be sulphur-shy. Spray when leaves are

size of shilling. Hand-picking of enlarged buds in winter is good way of destroying a lot. Very badly infested bushes should be burnt.

BLACK FLY : (See *Bean Aphis*.)

BLACKBERRY : Many cultivated varieties excellent for garden work. Strong growers, they should be trained up posts, trellises or wooden frames. Plant in autumn, first digging land well and incorporating manure. Allow about 8 ft. between plants. Propagate by tip-layering, that is pegging tips of young growths into soil in August. Prune established bushes after fruit has been picked each year. Remove growths which have borne fruits.

Varieties : *Himalayan Giant, John Innes.*

BLACKCURRANT : Easy fruit to grow. Dig soil well and deeply. Plant young bushes in November, cut back after Christmas to within 6 in. or so of the ground. Give dressing of fertilizer each year and top-dressing of manure. Prune established bushes after fruiting by cutting out old branches, to encourage development of young ones. One branch or so only should be removed according to vigour of each bush. Propagate by taking cuttings of soft green growths in May, and root in frame. Or take cuttings of young ripened wood in September, cut 8 or 9 in. long and leave on all buds. Plant out 9-in. apart in open garden and bury half their depth. If soil is heavy mix sand with it.

Varieties : *Boskoop Giant, Goliath, Baldwin.*

Pests : *Big Bud Mite, Aphis.*

Worst Disease : *Reversion.*

BLANCHING : If light is excluded from plants they are unable to form their natural green pigment and so remain white. Some plants are better for eating when blanched, as flavour is not so bitter, e.g., celery, leeks and endive.

BLIGHT : Term for a multitude of garden pests and ailments. Generally applied to epidemics, as when whole crop is attacked. Various forms of aphis are given the name. The worst potato disease is universally called Potato Blight. (See *Diseases* and *Pests*.)

◀ Mr. MIDDLETON says : *Won't it be grand when we can sit on*

BLIND : Plants which fail to produce flowers or to develop normally are said to be blind. Cauliflowers are prone to this producing four or five leaves, and no central bud which should give rise to more leaves in ordinary way. Single leaf usually occupies place of terminal bud, and such plants should be watched for, and discarded, when planting out.

BLOOD : This makes fine manure because rich in nitrogen, has little potash and some phosphoric acid. Can be used fresh, but should be dug into the soil deeply, as it will develop an offensive smell. Better dried, and can be purchased thus. Dissolved in water, makes excellent liquid manure. Used as top-dressing or liquid manure for plants in pots in greenhouse, it frequently develops harmless white fungus on top of soil.

BLUESTONE, or COPPER SULPHATE : Used to make Bordeaux mixture and other fungicides. Dusted on paths, can be used to kill weeds.

BOLTING : Gardener's term used when plants run up to seed, as with onions or beetroot, to detriment of edible part. Cauliflower heads also quickly bolt.

BONES AND BONE MEAL : Bones are rich in lime and phosphates, and make excellent phosphatic fertilizer. Crushed bones, ¼-in. size, useful for mixing into vine borders or orchards when soil is being prepared before planting. Contain fats and gelatine, and decay slowly, thus releasing food over period of years. When crushed they form coarse meal suitable for dressing on garden or mixing with potting soil. The food is then more readily available because of this fineness. Bones are rich in valuable gelatine and fats, which are nowadays generally removed and residue used as fertilizer. Bone meal, as purchased, has had the fats removed, while, when gelatine has been extracted, residue is sold as steamed bone flour. Bones are sometimes treated with sulphuric acid and sold as dissolved bones. Normal applications of bone meal or flour are 2–4 ozs. per square yard.

BORDEAUX MIXTURE : Fungicide, discovered accidentally in France last century, when bluestone was made into a wash and sprayed on vines to discourage stealing. Found that those sprayed suffered less than others from vine mildew. Ingredients are copper sulphate (bluestone), quick lime or hydrated lime, and water. To make, dissolve 1 lb. of bluestone in 8 gallons of water in a wooden (*not* metal) vessel. Slake 1 lb. quicklime by slowly adding water, and make into paste with 2 gallons water. Pour into bluestone solution through strainer. These quantities, 1–1–10, can be varied a little : increase lime for damaged plants. Bordeaux mixture spray is good control for many fungus diseases, e.g., *Celery Blight, Peach Leaf Curl, Apple Scab, Potato Blight.*

BORECOLE : (See *Kale*.)

BRASSICA : Cabbage family is the Brassica family. It includes such vegetables as cauliflowers, Brussels sprouts, Savoy cabbages, broccoli, kales. Also turnips, kohl-rabi, mustard, radish are brassicas.

BROCCOLI : Confusion often occurs over this vegetable. There are three types : the sprouting broccoli, which is grown for its young green shoots ; the Nine-Star form, which produces a number of small cauliflower-like heads ; and the heading type, which is really a winter or hardy cauliflower and is usually sold as cauliflower by greengrocer. Both broccoli and cauliflower are varieties of cabbage. Together they can provide succession whole year round in more genial parts of country. In north, broccoli is risky crop, but possible to have them up to Christmas. Selection of suitable varieties will give succession from October to June. **Autumn Varieties :** *Walcheren, Michaelmas White,* followed by *Veitch's Self-Protecting* and *Snow's Winter White* until Christmas. **Winter :** *Winter White, Winter Queen.* **Spring :** *Leamington, Eastertide,* followed by *Whitsuntide, Late Queen* and *Methven's June.* Pre-Christmas broccoli are raised on seed bed, seeds being sown in early April and plants put out in May. Later ones should be sown at suitable times until middle of May and transplanted in June or early July. All broccoli like firm ground, so it should be dug some time before planting. Later varieties are better on land not too rich or freshly manured. Anything which encourages soft growing reduces resistance to winter. To protect them in severe weather, heel them over towards north.

BRUSSELS SPROUTS : Fairly easy vegetable to grow, often spoiled through carelessness. Need deeply-dug soil which has had time to settle, plenty of nourishment while growing, and long season of growth. Sow seeds in mid-March for maincrop (earlier supplies can be obtained from sowings in February), in cold frame in north or outside in south. Plant when ready in early May, or if land is not ready, prick out and transplant later. Distances apart 2 ft. 6 in. each way, though later plantings can be put 2 ft. between rows. When using buttons remove bottom ones first. When cleared, tops can be used as late winter greens.
Varieties : *Darlington, The Wroxton, Fillbasket.*

BUDDING : Method of propagating fruit trees by inserting buds of selected varieties into stems of suitable rootstocks. Budding is done in summer.

BURGUNDY MIXTURE : A fungicide similar to Bordeaux mixture, and prepared in the same way, but washing soda is used instead of lime. Usual quantities are 1 lb. copper sulphate, 1¼ lb. soda, 10 gallons water.

BUSHEL : Dry measure, used for many fruits and vegetables. A bushel of soil occupies a box 22 by 10 by 10 in.

C

CABBAGE : A staple vegetable in our gardens. Seeds are sown in drills in seed bed from March onwards and will produce heads from July onwards. Varieties such as *Velocity* should be sown first, followed by *Utility* and *Winningstadt.* For winter work, *Christmas Drumhead* and *January King* will take succession to February. Plant out from April to July. Spring cabbage are sown last week in July or first week in August, and planted in September and October. Bolting is risk with earliest sowings. Suitable varieties are *Harbinger, Flower of Spring, Ellam's Early.* Distance between summer cabbage, large varieties, 2-ft. each way, smaller varieties 18 in. by 2 ft.
Pests : See *Cabbage Aphis, Cabbage Caterpillar, Cabbage Root Fly, Cabbage White Fly.*

CABBAGE LETTUCE : Ordinary type of lettuce as distinct from the upright growing cos lettuce. Resembles a cabbage in shape and way it hearts up.

CABBAGE APHIS : This pest is increasing. Attacks most members of brassica family. Grey mealy insect, generally found in clusters of many hundreds. Blotchy appearance of a cabbage leaf is sure sign of presence of colonies of insect on undersides of leaves. It passes the winter in the egg stage on the stems of Brussels sprouts, cabbage stumps, certain weeds, etc. When these hatch in spring, they spread to growing brassicas. Colonies resulting from initial infections may become so bad as to curl and distort plants and completely cripple them. To control, spray immediately with nicotine. When established in large clusters, pest is most difficult to clear completely.

CABBAGE CATERPILLARS : Life history of butterfly or moth begins when eggs are laid. These hatch and produce caterpillars (*larvæ*), which eat continuously until fully grown, when they turn into a pupa or chrysalis, wrapping themselves in a skin or cocoon. They next emerge as butterfly or moth, which begin circle again by laying eggs. You thus get eggs-larvæ-pupæ-adults-eggs. It is in larval or caterpillar stage that they are destructive. Cabbages and similar vegetables are attacked by caterpillars of three butterflies and two moths. They are large white, small white and green-veined butterflies,

◀ **Mr. MIDDLETON** says : *Keep quietly on without over-exerting*

Derris Dust Shaker

cabbage moth and garden pebble moth. Most important is large white butterfly, whose eggs are laid in clutches of a hundred; and when these hatch caterpillars are numerous enough to devour a large plant. Eggs of others are laid singly. The cabbage moth can be a nuisance, as caterpillar eats into heart of cabbage rather than feed on outer leaves. When butterflies are seen fluttering amongst green crops, plants should be examined frequently and any yellow eggs which are seen rubbed off. Should caterpillars appear, spray with derris. A spray made up with soft soap alone can be fairly effective. Derris is poisonous to caterpillars but not to humans, and should be sprayed on so as to cover leaves with film, both upper and lower surfaces.

CABBAGE ROOT FLY : Bad pest, not unlike house fly, which lays eggs in May in small batches at soil level near stems of brassica plants. They attack all members of cabbage family, especially cauliflowers. Also attack swedes, turnips, radishes, and even stocks. As impossible to catch adult fly, prevent it laying eggs. Deterrents such as naphthalene are fairly successful, if two or three applications made in May and early June. Calomel dust has come into vogue as control, but is rather expensive. Tarred felt discs, about 4-in. square, can be placed around stems and pressed flat on soil. These discs seem to be more effective if first dipped in calomel dust. Should a few plants show signs of flagging, and when pulled up have the white grubs eating into the stems, it is almost certain that most of crop has been attacked. It is practically impossible to kill grubs in soil, and only thing which has chance of doing so is corrosive sublimate (poison). Solution made by dissolving 1 oz. in 12½ gallons of water should be poured around plants. Two applications should be made. Also feed with nitrate of soda to stimulate growth.

CABBAGE WHITE FLY : Close relative of the aphis group of insects, and resembling greenhouse white fly. It attacks cabbages and allied crops, and is more usual in the south than the north. To control, spray with nicotine.

CALLUS : Tissue which forms at base of cuttings before roots develop.

CALOMEL DUST : Preparation containing small amount of mercury, which kills eggs of fly pests of plants. Has come into prominence during war, and has been used with fairly good effect against onion fly and cabbage root fly in particular. Unfortunately price has risen, so that it is scarcely economic proposition for small garden.

CANKER : Disease of apple and pear trees. Spores of fungus enter branch or twig at some suitable spot such as wound or leaf scar. They give rise to fungal threads which grow inside, and a slight depression is caused in the bark, which becomes progressively larger. As decay advances, an open wound is caused. This spreads until branch may be encircled and die. Diseased branches should be cut out and all pruning wounds painted. Trees should be fed with sulphate of potash, not with fertilizers containing nitrogen.

CAPSID BUGS : Three main species of capsid bugs are pests in gardens; two attack fruit trees, and the third garden plants, particularly potatoes. Fruit should be sprayed in winter with wash

yourself. That is the golden rule for all new gardeners. ▶

containing petroleum oil or with D.N.C. Eggs are buried in bark and have only cap showing. Ordinary tar-oil sprays are not very effective in destroying eggs.

CARABIDS : (See *Ground Beetles.*)

CARBONATE OF LIME : (See *Lime and Liming.*) Chemical name for ordinary natural chalk and limestone, which, though chemically identical, differ physically in that limestone is hard rock· while chalk is soft. Chalk is used on light soils, as it is, or ground into powder. Limestone is burnt in kilns to produce quicklime, and is slaked before spreading on land. Quicklime, or lump lime, absorbs water from ·air, generates considerable heat and breaks down into fine powder. This is known as slaking.

CARDOON : Vegetable not commonly grown. Grows to height of 4 ft. or more,. and has large deeply-cut leaves. Leafstalks are fleshy and white, and are edible. Seeds may be sown in March indoors, or in April outside where they are to grow. Inside, put two or three seeds in plant pot and reduce seedlings to one. Plant out in May after hardening off. Outside, sow on surface if soil is heavy, or in trenches if light. Seeds are put a few together at intervals of 2 ft. and later singled. Distance between trenches or rows is 3 ft. Feeding, watering and hoeing are main points in cultivation, until August, when plants are earthed up. Leaves are gathered together, wrapped with paper or straw, and banked with soil.

CARROT : Staple vegetable which is classified according to the size and shape of roots, as stump-rooted, short-horn, intermediate or long-rooted. First two are fairly quick growers. Seeds are sown at regular intervals from March to August to provide succession of young roots, and are often grown in frames during winter. Intermediate and long-rooted varieties are grown as maincrops for storage, being sown in April. Put seeds in drills 12 in. apart and sow thinly. To help thin sowing, seeds can be mixed with sand. Thin out the seedlings first to 2 in. apart and later to 6 or 7 in. Where carrot fly is nuisance in spite of attempts to control, shorter-rooted varieties should be grown, sown thinly and left unthinned, because smell of crushed leaves at thinning time attracts pests. Cultivation consists of occasional feeding with fertilizer and old soot, frequent hoeings in early stages but fewer later. In later stages, a little soil can be drawn around plants to prevent shoulders of roots from turning green. When tops take on metallic yellow appearance in October, lift plants on dry day and store unwashed roots in sand or clamp. On heavy soils· or where long roots are wanted for exhibition, holes can be bored in the soil at 9-in. intervals 2-in. across and 12-in. deep, filled with good soil, similar to that used for potting inside, and · rammed gently. A pinch of seed is sown at top of each hole and covered with soil. Later the ·seedlings are reduced to one.

Varieties : *SMALL-ROOTED FORMS —Scarlet Horn, Early Gem, Early Nantes; INTERMEDIATE FORMS — James Intermediate, Chantenay ; LONG-ROOTED FORMS—St. Valery, Altrincham, Long Red Surrey.*

Pests : (See *Carrot Fly.*)

CARROT FLY : Maggots of this fly, hatching from eggs laid on soil surface near plants, burrow and eat into roots of carrots. Flies appear in May and June and cannot be controlled by catching them. To keep flies away, use naphthalene hoed into soil between rows. Two or three dressings at 10-day intervals must be made. Spraying often with paraffin emulsion is reasonable control, while old soot dusted over plants is also deterrent. Where crop has been attacked, soil must be dug early so as to expose any pupæ to birds and frost.

CATERPILLAR : The larva or grub of butterfly or moth. (See *Cabbage Caterpillar.*)

CAULIFOWER : Member of brassica family grown for compact flower head. It is produced in summer as not hardy like broccoli. Soil for cauliflower should

outside or growing in a frame. Ordinary cucumbers are also grown easily in frames, and seeds should be sown now. Self-blanching celery is ideal for growing in cold frames after other seedlings have been used up. Seeds sown in boxes inside will come in for this purpose.

3. Plant First Leeks.—The first leeks should be planted now for those who are exhibiting or who like to have them early. Exhibitors must prepare their soil especially well, using manure and fertilizer. Leeks do like a rich soil. There are two ways of growing them— in trenches and in holes. The trench method is best for the exhibitor. It is made in the same way as a celery trench and is about 6-in. deep. The plants are put in 2- or 3-in. deep in single or double rows. As the plants grow they are earthed up with soil to produce well-blanched stems.

4. Cutting Asparagus.—Asparagus is now ready for cutting and must be done carefully. Special knives can be obtained for the work, but a good, long, narrow-bladed knife will serve. Cut the stalks when 4 or 5 in. long and insert the knife beneath the soil.

5. Sow Maincrop Beet.—Maincrop beet should be sown now, especially in the north. The long-rooted varieties in particular need a long season to develop. The globe forms will mature more quickly. Earlier sowings should be thinned out before they get overcrowded. In making sowings it is much better to sow continuously along the drill rather than in pinches at intervals, as with parsnips. If there is any failure of the seed, sowing in pinches often lets you down, whereas a continuous sowing usually provides enough to complete a row. Beet are better not transplanted, but blanks can be filled by carefully moving seedlings from one part of the row to another. Salsify sown earlier can be thinned to 6 in. apart.

6. Earth-up Potatoes ; Prepare Marrow Beds.—Potatoes growing should be kept earthed-up as they grow. Sites for vegetable marrows can be prepared.

They can be grown on heaps of soil and soil-covered shelters, but holes must be dug out 12 in. deep and 18 in. square, manure put in and some good soil to fill up. The trailing varieties are ideal for such positions.

7. Bark Ring Fruit Trees.—The bark ringing of over-vigorous fruit trees can be done any time from now till early June. A ring of bark ⅛-in. thick i taken out all round the trunk of the tree, or alternatively two half-rings, one above the other with about 4 in. between them and on opposite sides of the stem, are cut out. The purpose is to check the flow of elaborated food from the leaves down to the roots and to keep more of it in the branches. General growth is thus checked, as the surplus food in the branches has a tendency to congregate in the stronger buds and turn them into fruit spurs instead of shoots. The cuts should be covered with adhesive tape or painted.

8. Hunt Gooseberry Pests.—A common pest of gooseberries is the caterpillar of the magpie moth. Its presence is not always noticed until it has cleared much of the foliage. Examine the centre of bushes for attacked leaves, and if signs of the pest are there, spray with derris. Left unchecked they will destroy every leaf on the shrubs.

9. Sow, Plant and Hoe.—Make any necessary successional sowings. Prick out celeriac sown earlier. Dress shallots with fertilizer. Prepare outdoor tomato sites. Plant out parsley. Thin out salsify to 6 in. Hoe around fruit trees and bushes.

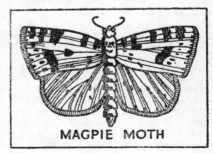

MAGPIE MOTH

If you don't know why you are cutting a shoot, don't cut it. ▶

Prick out 3-in. apart, and harden off for planting in May and June. Prepare trenches in late winter, digging them 18-in. deep and leaving them open for some weeks. Before planting put in good layer of farmyard manure, and fill with soil to within 10 in. of top. For single row trench should be 10–12-in. wide ; for double row, 18-in. wide. Plant firmly 12-in. apart. As plants grow, water and feed with liquid manure. When growth almost complete, begin to earth, building up soil 3 in. at a time once a week. Where possible first wrap with paper, to keep clean. Mix a little naphthalene with soil while earthing to discourage slugs. Cover plants almost completely, leaving only tops of leaves showing. In frosty weather put some straw over rows. There are self-blanching varieties of celery which are useful for early work. By planting them in batches 12 in. apart, they blanch each other without any necessity for earthing-up. They are particularly useful for growing in frames after spring seedlings are cleared, and can be used before frame is wanted for other purposes.

Varieties : *WHITE — Solid White, Superb White ; RED—Major Clarke's Red, Giant Red ; PINK—Aldenham Pink, Clayworth Pink, Standard Bearer.* (See *Celery Blight ; Celery Fly.*)

CELERY BLIGHT, or CELERY LEAF SPOT : Bad disease which attacks both celery and celeriac. It is seed-borne, and therefore seeds are generally treated with formalin before sale. Brown withered patches appear on leaves of attacked plants, and blight quickly runs through crop ; whole leaves wither and plants collapse. Only control is Bordeaux mixture, which must be sprayed on when first signs of disease appear. A number of other applications must be given. The blight may at first be confused with attacks of celery fly or leaf miner, but if patches are examined, tiny grubs will be seen in them.

CELERY FLY : Maggot of celery fly is leaf miner. Eggs are laid in celery leaf, and when they hatch, maggot eats

internal tissue. This forms yellow patches or blisters, and culprit will be found under skin. Best control is to keep fly away, so that it shall not lay its eggs. Frequent spraying with paraffin emulsion is useful, and so is dusting with 3 parts old soot and 1 part lime. When attack has taken place, grubs can be destroyed by squeezing yellow patches, tearing out small patches after squeezing so as to avoid going over them again later. Leaves may be forcibly sprayed with nicotine wash, particularly undersides. This is fairly effective against maggots, which are well protected inside the skin of the leaf.

CENTIPEDE : Creature with long body divided into many segments and having one pair of legs on each segment. Often confused with millipede, which has two pairs of legs on each segment, which makes it slow, while centipede is fast. Centipede is yellow or orange in colour, has strong biting mouth parts and feeds on insects, worms and other creatures in the soil. It is therefore beneficial and should not be destroyed. There are two main types in this country, one orange in colour, broad and strongly built, about an inch long or a little longer ; the other, known as the snake centipede, is more than 2-in. long, thin and yellow, and when seen seems to twist itself into knots.

CHALCID WASPS : Minute creatures, quite unlike true wasps, are mainly parasites, the larvæ living within the larvæ or pupæ of other insects. White fly parasite (*Encarsia formosa*), which keeps white fly in check, is an example.

CHALK (Carbonate of Lime) : The natural rock is quarried and dressed on light sandy soils in winter and allowed to weather. Valuable for increasing lime content of such soils. About 1–2 tons per acre is normal application. If put on at other times, should be purchased as powder. Chalk can also be turned into quicklime by burning.

CHARD : Blanched growths of globe artichoke, often used in autumn. Normally grown for edible flower heads.

◀ **Mr. MIDDLETON** says : *Happy, active bees mean good fruit crops.* ▶

CHERRY : Useful and beautiful fruit tree, which can only be accommodated in gardens of good size, as it is normally grown as a standard. Where there is a wall facing north, the *Morello Cherry* can be planted. The trees need at least 15 ft. of space, and should be fan-trained.

CHERVIL : Herb used to give flavour to salads, to soups, and as garnishing. Sow seeds in drills 12-in. apart, and thin the seedlings to 6 in.

CHESHUNT COMPOUND : Many plants are attacked in seedling stage by diseases which affect them at soil level. Whole boxes of seedlings may collapse. The disease is known as *Damping-Off.* Various fungi cause it. Best control is to water boxes of seedlings with *Cheshunt Compound,* made by mixing two parts copper sulphate with eleven parts ammonium carbonate and storing in tightly-corked bottle. Dissolve 1 oz. in 2 gallons of water to use.

CHICORY : Grown for leafy shoots, forced and blanched in winter. Sow seed outside in May in rows 15-in. apart. Thin seedlings to 9-in. apart. Hoe and feed occasionally in summer. Lift roots in autumn, cut tops to within an inch of root, and store in soil or sand in suitable corner. Take some and place close together, upright, in box of soil, and place under greenhouse bench or other warm place in dark. In about three weeks shoots can be cut.

CHIVES : Herb, member of onion family, which grows in tuft-like manner, similar to grass. Makes useful path edge and is used to flavour soups and stews. Seeds can be sown outside in March or April and thinned to 4/6-in. apart, or tufts can be divided and planted in March 6/9-in. apart. Clumps may remain for some years, but should be periodically lifted, divided and re-planted.

CHLOROPHYLL : The green colouring matter in the leaves of ordinary green plants. One of most vital substances on earth, as ultimately all life depends on it. By its means plants absorb energy from sun's rays and use it to manufacture elaborate foods from simple elements.

CLAMP : Also called pit, hog, bury, pie, and grave, and has other local names. Potatoes and other roots are stored out of doors by building them into conical heaps, covering them with good layer of soil, and then banking them up with soil. Digging soil out creates trench around clamp, and helps to drain it. Tufts of straw are allowed to stick through top ridge to act as ventilators. Cover with straw and leave for a day or two before soiling, so that roots will sweat. (See *Storage,* and diagram page 61.)

CLICK BEETLE : The parent stage of wireworms.

CLOCHE : From French intensive gardening. The word means " bell," and is now applied to glass cover of any shape. Modern cloche usually consists of flat glass sheets fastened together in simple wire frame to make miniature greenhouse or tent-shaped cover. These are placed end to end over rows of plants.

CLOVES : Name given to small bulbs which are really part of larger bulb, as with garlic or shallots.

CLUBROOT : Disease which attacks turnips, swedes, cabbage, broccoli, cauliflower, Brussels sprouts, mustard, radish, etc., and some ornamental plants. Known as a Slime Fungi. During part of life consists of single cell, capable of moving about in soil. These cells move in layers of moisture around particles of soil and when they chance upon root of suitable plant, force way inside. There they begin to multiply by dividing into twos, increase rapidly and irritate plant root into unconventional growth. Tissues swell, and swellings, if cut across, have mottled appearance and ultimately turn brown and rotten. They are sometimes confused with galls caused by turnip gall weevil, but the latter, if cut, contains grub or hole. Clubroot most common in acid or sour soils, so check by liming. Hydrated lime applied 1 lb. per square yard should be used, and put on during

◀ Mr. MIDDLETON says : *Don't bring seedlings on in rich soil,*

winter or early spring. If there is much clubroot in land, further dressings of ½ lb. per square yard should be put on during two succeeding years. It is wise to have soil tested for lime content at intervals. Your local adviser will do it for you or tell you where it can be done. On land infested with clubroot disease, a number of things should be considered. First, rotation of crops is important. Keep any of cabbage family away from bad pieces of land for some years, or cut down plantings of brassicas to minimum. Plants should be treated also with corrosive sublimate (mercuric bichloride), strong poison, which needs to be used with care. Dissolve 1 oz. in 12½ gallons water and apply to seedlings in seed bed at rate of 1 pint to every 5 ft. of row. When planting out, fill up holes with solution, and after planting, water in young plants with it. Avoid acid fertilizers, such as sulphate of ammonia, superphosphate, and dissolved bones. Substitute basic slag, nitrate of lime, and nitro-chalk. Diseased plants should be burned. Do not allow roots to decay in soil.

COCKCHAFER : Adult cockchafer is a beetle, often called the May bug, because found in May feeding on leaves of trees. Lay eggs in soil, and eggs hatch into grubs, which grow big feeding on underground parts of plants. Large, white and fleshy, with brown head, strong mouth parts, and three pairs of legs behind head. Latter end of body is legless, soft and fat. Normally in curled-up posture, and keep feeding for three years before turning into pupæ. Columns of this pest can be destroyed when digging, for they are easy to see. Naphthalene worked into soil is fairly effective against them. There are other smaller chafers, such as the summer chafer, the garden chafer, and the rose chafer.

COCKROACH : This pest is often nuisance in greenhouses, particularly harming seedlings. Trap by putting a little stale beer and sugar in jar and sinking almost to brim in floor. Poisoned bait made of Paris green ½ lb.,

bran 14 lbs., water 1 gallon, and a little treacle, can be used. Powdered borax is said to be effective if dusted around haunts.

CODLIN MOTH : Pest of apples. Adult moth lays eggs in May, singly, on or near young fruits. When caterpillars hatch, they bore into apple and feed inside. Attacked fruits often fall early. Pigs or poultry beneath trees will destroy grubs. From fruit which do not fall, larvæ emerge and look for suitable place to pupate. If hay bands are tied around stem, they will use these and can be destroyed later. Alternatively spray with derris wash when blossoms fade and so poison young caterpillars.

COLEWORT : Sometimes called a Collard. Name formerly applied to ordinary cabbage generally, but now restricted to very small type, which was perhaps forerunner of modern varieties. Useful small winter green. Sow in May or June and plant in July 12-in. each way, or sow where they are to grow and thin to 9-in. apart.

COLORADO BEETLE : Very serious potato pest in America, which has come to Europe, and spread rapidly. Not yet become established in this country, but extreme vigilance is needed so that any infection may be spotted and dealt with quickly.

COMPLETE FERTILIZER : Prepared, thoroughly-mixed fertilizer which contains three essential plant foods—nitrogen, potash and phosphates—in various proportions. Use of good, complete fertilizer is usually better than trying to mix your own. When buying always get statement of percentage of ingredients.

COMPOST : Has two meanings in gardening : (a) collection of garden refuse made into heap and rotted down for manure ; (b) mixture of soil and other ingredients specially prepared for potting purposes in greenhouse.

COMPOST HEAP : Farmyard manure has always been gardener's way of

and plant out in poorer soil. That is the wrong way round. ▶

enriching soil and maintaining fertility. Animal manures are scarce, and gardeners must find substitutes. Any material that will supply humus (see *Humus*) can be used. Spent hops straight from brewery or rotted down to make hop manure, peat, leaf-mould, straw, shoddy, sewage sludge, and slaughter-house refuse, are excellent materials. One of best ways of obtaining good humus-supplying material is to collect all garden and house refuse and rot it down in compost heap. Everything of plant origin will decay naturally, if left in casual heap. But this takes time, and the collection of refuse is offensive in appearance and smell. It may annoy neighbours and attract attention of sanitary authorities ! Better and inoffensive method is a proper compost heap, built up in such a way that decay is accelerated and smell is imprisoned. You can maintain and even increase fertility of your soil without buying farmyard manure, merely by saving all garden refuse and composting it, and supplementing it with fertilizers. If plot is newly broken from grass land, there will be enough reserve fertility in the soil to take you through first year if you dig in sods. During that year you can collect all your waste, rot it and dig it in during following winter. Various methods of compost-heap construction are recommended, but they are all basically the same. Rubbish is put in layers, and heap built up like series of sandwiches, using rubbish, soil, and other materials as alternating layers. Sort of materials and refuse suitable for rotting are tree leaves, grass mowings, vegetable leaves, plants that have run to seed, potato peelings, old straw, ordinary kitchen refuse, such as tea-leaves, egg shells, carpet sweepings, in fact, anything that will decay. Soft hedge clippings can be included, though not long woody ones. Potato haulms and pea and bean tops are also useful. Weeds and faded flowers and old plants can be included. Wood or wooden stems should not be included, but green stems, such as tomato and cabbage stalks, are suitable

if chopped up. The following description gives the method of constructing simple type of compost heap. Choose spot in shade, but not too near house. Dig out a pit, 9-in. deep (the depth of the surface soil), 5-ft. long and 4-ft. wide. This is large enough for the amount of rubbish obtained from ordinary garden. Pile soil around side. Put layer of rubbish in pit about 12-in. thick, mix well, and break any stemmy material. If dry, wet thoroughly to help decay, preferably with liquid manure. Put layer of soil 1-in. thick on rubbish. This helps to absorb acids produced as material rots, and so speeds decomposition. If you are lucky enough to have a little ordinary manure to spare, place layer 2/3-in. thick on top of refuse and underneath soil. This helps decay and enriches material. Small amount of hydrated lime can be dusted on soil. On top of this place another layer of rubbish 6/9-in. thick, following again with soil or manure and soil. Repeat process until heap is from 3/4-ft. high, each layer being slightly narrower than previous, thus forming sloping sides. These sides should be banked with a 2/3-in. thickness of soil, and heap finished off neatly and left to decay. It will shrink considerably ; but do not pack too tightly, as the more air that circulates through heap the quicker its decay. Be sure to keep it damp and sprinkle a little lime on it occasionally to prevent smell. Two things indicate well-made compost heap : (1) weed should not grow on it ; (2) material, when fit for mixing with the soil, should be uniformly dark in colour and have pleasant earthy smell. Such a heap can be as rich as farmyard manure. (See illustrations on pages 7 and 66.)

CORDON : Specialised form of fruit tree, trained and pruned to single stem. Term also used for training of any plants on single stem, as with sweet peas.

CORN, SWEET (or MAIZE) : Tender plant more suited to cultivation in the south than in the north. In difficult areas seeds should be sown, in greenhouse in early April, either singly in pots or in boxes. Can be planted out when hardened off in May. In some areas, seeds can be sown outside in May. Set the seeds 6-in. apart in rows 2-ft. apart and thin to 12 in. Water in dry weather and feed occasionally. *Golden Bantam* is suitable variety.

CORN SALAD, or LAMB'S LETTUCE : Native of Britain, and grown as salad. Sow during August in drills 12-in. apart ; thin seedlings to 6 in.

CORROSIVE SUBLIMATE (Mercuric bichloride) : Dangerous poison. Handle with great care and do not leave about. One of the best controls of clubroot disease and root fly of cabbage. The proportions are 1 oz. to $12\frac{1}{2}$ gallons of water.

CRANE FLY, or DADDY LONG LEGS : Adult of leatherjacket. Soil pest.

CRESS : Ordinary cress can be grown easily by sowing seeds on boxes of soil, on borders in warm greenhouse in winter, or outside in summer. Usually cut when about 2-in. high. Succession easy to get by series of small sowings.

CROPPING PLAN : All wise gardeners plan their crop lay-out well in advance of any planting or seed sowing. This is only way for maximum results, and it gives guidance on amounts of seed to order. Draw plan of outline of garden to scale, say, 1/10th in. to 1 ft. (see notes for beginners, page 12). Divide into three roughly equal portions (see *Rotation of Crops*). In one group have all green crops, in another potatoes and roots, and in last peas, beans and miscellaneous crops. Draw lines across plan to indicate where crops will grow. For instance, if you are to grow two rows of dwarf peas, two of dwarf kidney beans, and two of broad beans, this will mean six rows each 2-ft. apart. Decide where you will place them in garden, then draw lines across plan 2/10ths in. apart, to indicate where they are to go. Similarly with all crops according to distances they are to be apart, and write in the name of each one. Run all rows from north to south as near as your garden permits. Study the sample cropping plan on pages 50 and 51 and adapt to requirements.

By arrangement with Ministry of Agriculture and Fisheries, we are able to present with this book a copy of the Ministry's Cropping Plan. Study this also.

CROSS-FERTILIZATION : Fertilization of the female organs of one flower by the pollen from another. Often happens naturally, pollen being transported by wind or insects. But some flowers are always fertilized by pollen from themselves. In plants, like tomatoes, grown for fruits, Nature has often to be helped owing to artificial circumstances of growth, and rabbit's tail is usually used. With hardy fruits, such as apples, modern varieties are so complex that pollen from their own flowers or from other trees of same kind is often useless. Therefore mixed planting of varieties is necessary.

CROWN : Perennial rootstock of any plant, such as rhubarb, is often called a crown, as is main plant of strawberry.

CUCUMBER : Staple article of diet in Russia and elsewhere in Europe. In Britain is grown chiefly for salad. Ordinary type must be cultivated in greenhouse or frame. Sow seeds singly in small pots around March, and keep in temperature of 65° F. As seedlings grow, pot into larger pots and give some support like small cane to which to tie growth. Prepare bed either on floor or on bench of heated house. Mix soil by using good loam, well-rotted manure, some leaf-mould, a little sand, and some general fertilizer. Build into heaps about 6/9-in. high and 2-ft. apart. Plant on these. Wires should be run horizontally along house a foot apart, to which growths can be tied. Allow main stem to run to top of greenhouse, then stop it. Side shoots will be produced in axils of leaves, and should be trained sideways and tied to wires. Stop them at second leaf, allow one cucumber to grow from first leaf, and a cucumber and another stem from second. This stem is again stopped at second leaf,

and so on as far as they grow. Allow side growths to overlap, but keep tied in to wires. Ridge cucumbers can be grown out of doors in sunny spots. Sow in April indoors, and plant in early June either on good soil heaps or in specially prepared positions.

CUTWORMS : Among commonest of soil pests are cutworms or larvæ of certain moths. The turnip moth, hart and dart moth, and the yellow underwing moth are most common species. Prevalent all over country, caterpillars are dirty grey in colour and are found while digging. Do much damage, feeding on stems of plants, both below and above ground, hence their other name of surface caterpillar. You must keep your garden clear of weeds even when crop is finished, as weeds attract moths when egg-laying. Picking out grubs when digging is one of best methods of control. If there is very bad infestation, use poison bait. A mixture of 1 lb. Paris green (*arsenic oxide*) with 25 lb. of bran, moistened slightly and broadcast sparingly over surface, will kill many. This is dangerous poison and must be used with care.

D

DAMPING OFF : Various fungi attack seedlings and young plants at soil level and cause them to collapse. To control, water with *Cheshunt Compound* (which see).

DAMSON : Fruit popular for jam-making and preserving. Culture is same as for plums.

DERRIS : The powdered rootstock of tropical plants, which contains ingredient (rotenone) poisonous to cold-blooded creatures, but not to man. Hence its suitability as insect poison on food plants.

DEVIL'S COACH-HORSE BEETLE : Recognisable by its habit of raising its tail when checked or threatened. It is a large insect and is beneficial, because it preys on other insects.

DIBBER : A piece of wood used for making holes in soil in which to place the roots of plants. They range from small pencil-like pieces for small seedlings to large two-handed tools for potatoes.

DIE-BACK : Name for number of diseases of trees and bushes. Branches die back, starting usually at tip. Affected branches should be cut out and the wound painted. See to drainage and feed plants with potash to strengthen them.

DIGGING : Good digging is foundation of good gardening. Should be done as early as possible in winter, particularly with heavy soils. Only lightest soils should be left until spring. First divide plot in halves lengthwise, by putting line down centre. Then take out trench 12/15-in. wide, spade-deep (10 in.) across end of one half. Clean out all crumbs and leave sides as straight as possible. Wheel or throw soil on path near untouched half of garden. Begin to dig by turning over strip of soil 12/15-in. wide into trench, thus creating another trench exactly the same size. If you wish to do job thoroughly you can measure each width. Clean out all crumbs and place them on top. Proceed thus until you reach end of plot. You will be left with trench, which can be filled from first trench on the other half of garden ; this will let you work back to end from which you started. Here soil on path from original trench can be used to fill last trench, and so complete job. Width and depth of trench must be kept same all through, to get perfect level. If there is turf or rough grass and weeds on your land, skim them and place face downwards in bottom of each trench and chop into small pieces. They will soon decay. Do not skim and stack turf unless it contains troublesome weeds or you need it for greenhouse work. This is simple digging. Better is double digging. Trench must be at least 2-ft. wide and be kept to same width right through operation. All crumbs must be cleaned out and placed on top of turned-over soil to ensure complete reversal. Bottom of trench is then broken up with digging fork. It is worth while even if subsoil is very heavy clay and difficult to loosen. If plenty of manure, or other organic materials such as peat, leaf-mould or compost is available, scatter on bottom of trench and fork in. This is particularly valuable in preparing onion bed. Should your land be grassland, a strip of turf 2-ft. wide should be skimmed off as described above, placed upside-down in trench, and chopped small. The 2-ft. strip of soil is then turned over on to chopped turf. Work with your left side to trench, moving backwards down strip. The crumbs are again cleaned out and sides of trench straightened off. Cycle then begins again. Whole plot is done in this way, and last trench is filled with soil from first trench as with simple digging. This double digging is essential in first year. Subsequently it need only be done every third year except for special crops, such as onions. If you have manure, compost material or other organic matter, use judiciously, working some into each trench as you dig. If, however, you have planned garden correctly, you will know where your different crops are to be. This will enable you to avoid putting fresh manure where your root crops, such as carrots, beet and parsnips, will be grown. These do better on ground not freshly manured. (See *Bastard Trenching*.)

DISEASES : Plant diseases are of three main types : (1) those caused by attacks of fungi which live as parasites on plants, and include bacteria ; (2) virus diseases ; and (3) those caused by some natural process such as drought, frost, lack of certain foods, etc., and known as physiological diseases. Fungi diseases are most important. They cannot manufacture own food out of salts from soil, so feed on green plants. Usually enter through wound, perhaps caused accidentally by tool, or made by insect or by weather, and often they enter through breathing pores in leaves of plants. Once inside, their threads grow and spread, permeating cells, feeding on contents. These cells die and so you get obvious signs of disease. Fungi

You don't get on any faster, but merely make hard work of it. ▶

mainly reproduce themselves by means of tiny bodies called spores. These often produced in millions, and when ripe float in air and are borne by winds to other plants, which they infect. Only two substances known for killing these fungi are copper and sulphur. All remedies contain one or other in some form. Sometimes possible to check these diseases, for instance, by liming soil. Sterilization of soil is also useful. (See *Anbury, Bacteria, Bordeaux Mixture, Cheshunt Compound, Die Back, Onion Mildew, Peach-Leaf Curl, Reversion, Scab Disease, Silver Leaf, Virus Disease.*)

D.N.C. : (*Dinitro-ortho-cresol.*) Modern winter-spray fluid for fruit trees.

DRILL : Small trench or furrow made with hoe or spade to receive seeds.

DRY-ROT DISEASE OF POTATOES : Disease of potatoes which occurs in storage. Tubers wrinkle and shrink, wrinkles being in concentric rings. Grey spots are seen on affected parts. Chiefly important on seed potatoes : affected tubers usually decay in soil. They should be destroyed.

E

EARTHING UP : Drawing of soil around potato plants, around many other vegetables, such as celery and leeks, in order to produce white stems, and also around stems of late cabbage, Savoys, etc., to protect them in winter.

EARTHWORMS : Essential to well-being of soil. Their burrowing drains and aerates soil. Feed on leaves and dead vegetation and much soil passes through their stomachs and gets well broken up. Deposit casts on surface, bringing soil and plant foods from below to top. This helps to improve physical condition of soil.

EARWIG : Very destructive pest, feeding on the leaves, flowers and particularly fruits of plants. Eggs are laid in soil in autumn in batches of 50 or so, and female remains near until young emerge in spring. Adults feed at night, going into hiding during day. By providing attractive hiding places for them many can be destroyed. Inverted flower pot on cane with hay or straw in it is good trap. Examine traps frequently, each day if possible. Bamboo canes and broad bean stalks are also good traps. A successful poison bait is made as follows : 4 lbs. bran, 1 pint black treacle, ½ lb. sodium fluoride, and 1 gallon of water. Bait is chiefly useful in greenhouse.

EELWORMS : Tiny microscopic worms ; many live within tissues of plants and cause much trouble. Thread-like creatures seen in soil are not eelworms : eelworm is invisible to naked eye, except for females when swollen with eggs. Many varieties of eelworms, often named after plants they attack, e.g., Potato Eelworm which causes potato sickness. *Stem Eelworm* and *Root-Knot Eelworm* are serious pests in greenhouses, but can be controlled by sterilizing soil. Gardens more difficult to sterilize, and where potato eelworm is present, potatoes should not be grown there for number of years.

ENDIVE : Useful salad for autumn and winter use when lettuce is scarce. Successive sowings are made from late June to early September. Sow seed on special outdoor bed ; transplant seedlings 12-in. apart in rows also 12-in. apart. Need rich, well-dug soil. Leaves must be blanched for eating, by covering with a box or pot when endives fully grown. Do not use flat pieces of wood or slate directly on the plants. Early sowings will mature out of doors, but later ones should be lifted in October, and transferred to cold frame to finish. Two main types are *Moss-Curled,* for early use, and *Batavian,* for winter supplies.

ESPALIER FRUIT TREES : Fruit trees with branches trained horizontally from main upright stem and spaced out equally. Apples and pears are chief fruits so grown. Used as fences, or along paths in kitchen garden, or for growing against walls. Branches are tied to wires, and growths are vigorously pruned.

◀ Mr. MIDDLETON says: *The later you sow, the deeper seeds should be.* ▶

F

FARMYARD MANURE : Now in very short supply. Consisting of manure from all farm animals, mixed with plenty of straw and other litter, it is ideal material for enriching soil. Chief value is that it increases humus content, though it contains fair proportion of plant foods. Should be used whenever it can be obtained, but necessary now to use some substitutes. (See *Compost Heap, Green Manuring*.)

FERTILIZER : Artificial manures. Chemical compounds are purchasable as dusts or powders for supplying foods to plants. Three important plant foods normally lacking in soil are nitrogen, potash and phosphates. Various substances and compounds are obtainable which will make good these deficiencies. Buy good compound manure containing all three foods, such as the *National Growmore Fertilizer*.

FINGER AND TOE : (*Clubroot Disease*, for which see p. 90.)

FISH MANURE : Fish waste dried and sold as manure is very good fertilizer. Can be dug into the soil untreated, but smell is offensive.

FLEA BEETLE : Tiny black beetles, usually about 1/10th-in. long. Many species. Called flea beetles because of habit of jumping. Difficult to see, but damage they do to turnip and beet seedlings is obvious. They bite holes in leaves and sometimes completely destroy seedlings. When signs of attack seen, dust plants with derris powder. Naphthalene can be hoed in at sides of rows as deterrent.

FORMALDEHYDE AND FORMALIN : Formaldehyde is gas which, dissolved in water, is known as formalin. A 40 per cent. solution is of value for sterilising soils and to clean down greenhouses. Stings eyes, so apply carefully.

FUMIGATION : Use of vapours, smoke and gases to kill insect pests, chiefly in greenhouses. Various gases are used, such as hydrocyanic acid gas, naphthalene, and tetrachlorethane. Soils

can also be fumigated by using gases as carbon bisulphide.

FUNGICIDE : Substances used to kill fungi. Most important contain copper or sulphur in one form or another. Examples are *Bordeaux mixture*, lime-sulphur, potassium sulphide, copper sulphate, flowers of sulphur, *Cheshunt compound*.

G

GARLIC: Member of onion family greatly favoured in southern Europe as food. In Britain, used mainly for flavouring. Taste is strong, and smell pungent. Bulb is split into separate scales called " cloves." These cloves are planted in April, being pushed into soil 2-in. deep and 6/9-in. apart in rows 1-ft. apart. Hoeing and weeding are only cultivations necessary. Lift when leaves turn yellow, leave in sun to dry, and store like onions.

GENERAL FERTILIZER : Fertilizer which contains all the important plant foods for general use. (See *Fertilizer*.)

GOOSEBERRY : Easily-grown fruit bushes which will succeed on most soils. Plant November in open, sunny position sheltered from winds, 4½/5-ft. apart. Gooseberries can be grown as single-stemmed cordons and trained up walls and fences. Plant these 12-in. apart. First pruning after planting is important and is done before growth begins in spring. If bush is two or three years old and has four or five stems, cut these back to half to give foundation to future bush. Older and established shrubs are spur-pruned. Crowded shoots in centre are cut out, main shoots or leaders are tipped, while lateral growths are cut back to two buds. Where birds peck out buds in winter leave pruning until just before growth begins again. Give annual dressings of general fertilizer at about ½ lb. per bush, and mulch in spring with farmyard manure. Pick proportion of fruits while small and use for cooking and preserving. Leave few to mature and ripen fully for dessert. Propagate by taking cuttings 10-in. long of current year's wood in September

and October. Remove all buds except top five and plant out 9-in. apart.

Pests : *Magpie Moth* (for which see p. 104) ; *Gooseberry Sawfly*, and the *Gooseberry Aphis*.

Diseases : *Gooseberry Mildew* and *American Gooseberry Mildew*.

GRAFTING : Propagation of fruit trees by putting short hardwood cuttings on to stems of specially-grown rootstocks. These rootstocks are selected for their vigour. By grafting on to one of poor vigour, dwarf trees are obtained, suitable for cordons or growing in pots. By using a strong rootstock, standard and half-standard trees are produced. Similar stocks of medium vigour are used to produce bush forms. There are various methods of grafting cuttings or scions on to stocks. Rejuvenation of old trees can be done by grafting, putting new varieties on framework of trees. Commonest way of joining graft or scion to the rootstock is known as " whip-and-tongue " grafting. Root-stock is first bought, planted in November, and allowed at least a year to establish itself. During winter, before grafting, prunings of healthy twigs of selected varieties are picked out, and heeled-in together in sheltered part of garden. In March grafting is begun. Cut back stock, which will be about 1/1½-in. across, to within approximately 1 ft. of ground. Make clean cut with secateurs straight across. Take suitable piece of twig, which will be at least ¼-in. across, and cut it to 6 in. Make at bottom end long slanting cut 1½-in. long. Knife should be sharp, and one cut should be enough to produce clean, unfrayed surface. Next make cut on stock equal in size to that on scion. Place together to see that they are roughly identical. Two may be bound together thus, but are apt to be easily loosened. To prevent this, make tongue by cutting an incision ¼-in. deep and ½-in. from tip of cut surface of scion. Make similar incision on stock so that tongue is also produced. Fit scion to stock, and two tongues will provide firm hold which rough weather will not loosen.

◀ **Mr. MIDDLETON** says : *There's nothing to be gained by rushing*

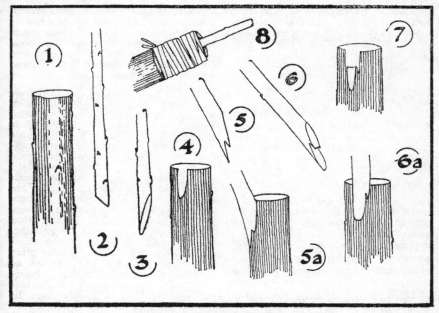

THE ART OF GRAFTING

(1) *Rootstock, cut back with secateurs:* (2) *Graft of scion of chosen variety:* (3) *Slanting cut at base of scion:* (4) *Stock with cut of equal size:* (5) *and* (6) *Scion cut to form tongue:* (6a) *The two joined:* (7) *Tongue cut on stock:* (8) *Joint finished.*

Fasten tightly with adhesive tape or raffia, and paint over with grafting wax. Later, when scion and stop have grown together, raffia and wax are removed. Whip-and-tongue method can be used when "frame-working" established trees. All side shoots and spurs are removed, leaving only bare framework of tree. Scions of requisite variety are then attached to main stems by whip-and-tongue method. There are many other ways of grafting, such as the Cleft, Rind, Crown methods, but they are not within the scope of this Guide.

GREASEBANDS : Certain moths, caterpillars of which damage fruit trees, have females which are wingless. To lay eggs in tree tops, these females must climb trunk. Greasebands are way of trapping them. Grease must be of type which always remains sticky, does not melt in sun, nor set hard in frosty weather. Spread on 6-in. width of greaseproof paper tied around trunk.

GREENFLY : (See *Aphis.*)

GREEN MANURING : Useful method of manuring soil is to grow a crop specially for the purpose of digging in. Crop is sown usually after a vegetable has been cleared, such as early potatoes. Mustard is valuable for purpose, as it is a leafy crop and seed is cheap. Sow in spring, allow to grow to nice size, but not to flower, and then dig into soil. For sowing in autumn to be dug in in spring, rye, tares, or turnips are most suitable.

out with a spade and turning everything upside down in a few hours.▶

GROUND BEETLES (or *Carabids*): Beneficial insects living mainly on other insects. Only troublesome when adults go for strawberries, and then easily trapped by putting a little meat in jar and sinking it to the brim in soil. Larvæ are carnivorous and do much good. Unfortunately, sometimes mistaken for wire worms and destroyed.

GUANO : South American name for bird droppings.

H

HALF-HARDY : Term applied to plants, usually grown in garden during summer, which will not survive winter out of doors.

HALF-STANDARD : Form of fruit tree usually having main trunk from 4/5-ft. high.

HARDY : Plants which will stand winter out of doors.

HARICOT BEANS : (See *Bean, Haricot*.)

HAULMS : Stems or stalks, and applied particularly to peas, beans and potatoes.

HEELING-IN : Temporary planting of plants, shrubs or trees when received from nurseryman. Saves unnecessary exposure of roots by lying about until plants can be dealt with. For smaller shrubs and plants, trench is taken out roughly on vacant piece of land. They are placed in close together, soil is put over roots and pressed down with foot. Larger subjects are placed singly in roughly-dug holes.

HOES AND HOEING : Push or Dutch hoe is one of most important tools. Not only destroys weeds but has other useful attributes. For instance, by loosening surface soil it helps to prevent loss of moisture in dry periods. Also distributes bacteria about soil, and so, with nitrifying bacteria, helps to increase nitrogen available to plants. Hoeing, therefore, is worth doing well. Many people make the mistake of hoeing forward. You should always hoe backwards. Stand on unhoed soil loosening portion in front of you, throwing weeds forward, and walk slowly backwards as you work. Never stand on ground already loosened. When hoeing out weeds, make sure that they are completely loosened and, if possible, turn them over with the roots facing upwards. If weather is dry, you may leave them there to die, but if showery rake off. Do not just push against the weeds and leave them to grow again. Take care when hoeing not to damage plants. Even slight damage done in this way can create wound which will admit bacteria and plant may be crippled or die. Useful push hoe is known as the Sproughton hoe, with which you can work between plants easily as well as down the rows, without having to turn half sideways. To loosen soil thoroughly, hoe should be inserted about ½ to 1 in. deep into soil and pushed along underneath surface, loosening soil completely. The hoe is taken out and inserted into soil again 8/9 in. further back and pushed forward until it cuts through to previous insertion. This makes completely loosened layer on surface. Do not insert hoe too deeply, as plant roots may be cut, one of dangers of too frequent hoeing. Drag hoe is used for many purposes, such as earthing-up and drawing drills. Also effective in breaking up lumpy land and destroying weeds. In using it against weeds, unlike push hoe, you must work forward, chopping out weeds and pulling them towards you, standing on work you have done. Drag hoe never completely loosens soil without tearing lumps out, and there is also danger of going too deep and cutting plant roots.

HORSE-RADISH : Easily-grown plant. Pieces of thick root 3-in. long are planted in February, 15 by 9 in. apart. Push roots 3/4 in. down. Better to replant each year than to abandon corner of garden to it.

HOT-BED : Heap of fresh manure so arranged that heat generated can be used to grow plants. Manure and leaves mixed, or dried leaves alone, will serve. Normally heap is 2/3-ft. high and large enough to carry frame.

◀ Mr. MIDDLETON says : *When you are getting flabby and*

Tread reasonably firm, and put on frame with 6/9-in. layer of soil inside. Seeds are sown, and light put over the top. Seedlings can be brought on quickly in this way, and out-of-season crops of carrots, turnips, etc., be obtained. Cucumbers and melons can also be grown on hot-bed.

HOVER FLIES : Large flies so named because they hover perfectly still in air. Beneficial as larvæ feed on aphids.

HUMUS : Residue of decayed remains of plants and animals in soil. When organic matter of any description, such as straw, leaves, manure, etc., is added to soil it slowly decays, ultimately losing original shape and becoming moist black substance. This is humus, vital constituent of soil.

HYDRATED LIME : (See *Lime*.)

I

ICHNEUMON FLIES : Large group of insects, parasitic on other insects and therefore beneficial.

K

KAINIT : Valuable potash fertilizer normally obtained from Germany and France, where it is mined. Contains several salts and also a percentage of sulphate of potash. Apply to land in winter before crops are set out, to permit impurities to be washed out.

KALES : Sometimes called *Borecole*. Hardy greens of which there are many forms grown for human consumption. Best are Curled or Scotch kale, Cottager's kale, Asparagus kale, and Drumhead kale. Sow seeds out of doors in April, and transplant 2 ft. by 2 ft. in final positions in May and June, or as late as July.

KIDNEY BEAN : (See *Bean*.)

KOHL RABI, or *Kohl Kohl* : Frequently called turnip-rooted cabbage, but is really turnip-stemmed cabbage. Edible part is not swollen root like turnip, but compressed swollen stem, which makes excellent vegetable. Cultivation is similar to that of turnip. Sow in drills

12-in. apart in April or May, and thin to 9-in. apart. Use when half-grown before becoming coarse.

L

LACEWINGS : Delicate flies with green wings. Beneficial because larvæ feed on green flies and similar pests.

LADYBIRD : Familiar beetles, beneficial both as larvæ and adults. Feed on green flies, scale insects, leaf hoppers, etc. Larva known as " nigger."

LAMB'S LETTUCE : (See *Corn Salad*.)

LAYERING : Method of propagation of new plants. Branches or side growths are partially severed, pegged down into soil until rooted, and then severed. Strawberries lend themselves naturally to layering.

LEAD ARSENATE : Poison used to kill biting insects. Applied as spray, usually 1 oz. to 1 gallon of water. Dangerous poison and must be handled with care. Must not be applied to food crop just before use, or on plants where bees are working.

LEADER : Year's growth of fruit-tree branch or stem which is a continuation of main branch. Not a lateral.

LEAF MINERS : Various insects lay eggs in plant leaves, and larvæ tunnel through tissues of leaf. Difficult to control once inside, as leaf skin protects them. Apply suitable deterrent to plants to keep fly away, e.g., paraffin emulsion.

LEATHER-JACKETS : Larvæ of the daddy-long-legs or crane fly. Pest in lawns and sometimes troublesome among vegetables on newly-broken land.

LEEK : Vegetable of onion family of fairly easy culture. Suffers from few diseases, is hardy and matures during winter. Seeds sown February to April, the earliest inside, later ones on outdoor seed bed. Plant in rows 12-in. apart with 9 in. from plant to plant. Usual method is to make hole 6/9-in. deep, and 2-in. across, and drop young plants in after trimming leaves. Plants are

fifty-ish, you don't swing a stockaxe quite so easily as you used to do. ▶

SECRETS OF SUCCESS WITH YOUR LEEKS

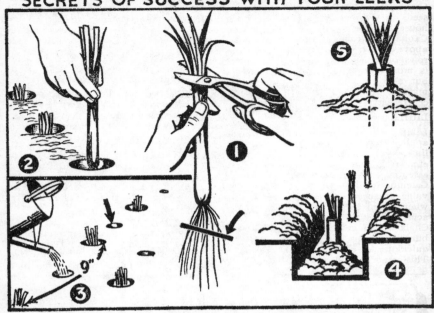

1. *Leaves and roots trimmed back.* 2. *Holes 8" to 10" deep made with dibber.*
3. *Watered in, but the hole is not filled in.* 4. *Trench method of planting.*
5. *Earthing up.*

watered only, hole not being filled in. For exhibition purposes, generally grown in trenches 6-in. deep, and earthed up as they grow to obtain good length of white stem.

Varieties : *Musselburgh, The Lyon, Prizetaker.*

LEGUME : Name given to all pod-bearing plants such as peas and beans, from natural order—*Leguminoseæ.*

LETTUCE : Valuable salad, easy to produce. Succession can be obtained all the year round by using frames and cloches in winter. First sowing made in January in greenhouse in boxes of soil. Prick seedlings into other boxes, harden off gradually and plant in open garden. Sow again in February and March, planting outside until May.

Good varieties for these sowings are *All the Year Round, Webb's Wonderful, Borough Wonder.* Make sowing in open garden in April, and thin out seedlings ; from then until August sow at intervals of fortnight. Transplanting in summer is not generally good as plants are difficult to establish in dry weather. Varieties for summer culture are *Continuity, All the Year Round, Market Favourite.* For autumn lettuce sow in July and early August, and thin to 9-in. apart. For winter lettuce sow in late August and plant out in September. These will need cloche protection in some parts, or should be planted in cold frames. Seeds sown in September can be grown in cold greenhouses. Varieties for winter, outside, are *Stanstead Park, May King, Arctic King* ; for

◀ **Mr. MIDDLETON says :** *Old brick dust. or mortar rubble, from*

greenhouse culture, *Cheshunt Early Giant*, *Gotte-a-forcer*, *Tennis Ball*. Sow seeds in October in frames and greenhouse for late winter and spring crop. Cabbage lettuce varieties mentioned above are good for intercropping between rows of other vegetables. Cos lettuce is more upright than cabbage lettuce, but also easy to grow. When nearly mature, tie round middle to blanch centre leaves.

LIGHT : Glass top of frame.

LIME : Word used for all forms of lime applied to soil, such as quicklime, waste lime, hydrated lime, carbonate of lime, etc. Also used for calcium, which is essential element of these substances. Calcium itself is plant food, but real value of these lime substances is that when added to the soil they react with acids and neutralise them (see *Acid Soil*). Chalk and limestone are quarried and burned in kilns, resulting product being quicklime, or burnt lime and lump lime. This absorbs water up to about half own weight and yet remains dry. As it absorbs moisture, great heat is generated and lime falls into fine powder, known as slaked or hydrated lime. Lime should be in fine state of division to get perfect mixing with soil. This is real value of slaked quicklime over other forms. Unfortunately often spoiled by bad slaking, being left until like putty or has set rather hard again. Slake quicklime by sprinkling with water, and then spread over garden. Usual quantity is $\frac{1}{2}$ lb. per square yard, or 1 ton per acre. Lime helps by neutralising acidity, by breaking up heavy soils and making easier to work, by releasing certain plant foods locked up in soil, and by discouraging soil pests.

LIME-SULPHUR : Mixture of lime and sulphur used against certain insect pests and many fungus diseases of plants. Normally bought as proprietary article owing to difficulties of mixing at home.

LIQUID MANURE : Animal urine and waste collected in tanks at farms is

a demolished building, is excellent stuff for heavy clay soil. ▶

Make liquid manure by putting farmyard manure in sack and immersing in water

richest form of liquid manure. Drainage from manure heaps is fairly good. Liquid manure for feeding crops can be made up by filling a sack with manure and hanging in tub of water. Do not put manure in water, as it clogs watering cans. Fertilizers, such as dried blood and most general artificials, can be dissolved in or mixed with water and applied to plants.

LIVER OF SULPHUR (Potassium sulphide): Remedy for many plant diseases, replaced to some extent by lime-sulphur. Can be purchased as solution and diluted for spraying, which is the best way, or can be bought in dry lumps and dissolved in water. Against various rust diseases, such as bean rust, blackberry rust, and raspberry rust it is good control. If used in greenhouse, stains woodwork.

LOAM: Soils intermediate between sand and clay are termed loams. Word also used for soil made from turf specially stacked for use in greenhouse work.

LOGANBERRY: Popular fruit, supposed to be a hybrid of raspberry and blackberry, and ideal for cooking and preserving. Plant is robust and strong, growing as much as 15 ft. in a year. Will thrive in odd corner, and can be used to cover walls or fences. If not grown against fence, wooden trellis must be erected for support. Propagation is by tip-layering (see *Layering*).

Plant in November or March, 8/12-ft. apart. Dig deep holes 2/3-ft. square, break up sub-soil, work in some manure, cover roots with good soil, and do not bury too deeply or damage any of the growth buds showing on root. Cut back to within 15 in. of ground after planting. Subsequent pruning consists of cutting out fruited wood after fruit has been picked, and tying in young growths to framework. Apply dressing of general fertilizer each year about ½ lb. per plant.

LOGANBERRY BEETLE: This beetle appears in May, lays eggs in blossoms of loganberry, and larvæ hatch and bore into the fruits. To control, spray twice with derris at flowering time.

M

MAGPIE MOTH: Pest of gooseberries and currants. Adult moths are rather striking, having wings of creamy-white with black spots, and some orange marks. Eggs are laid in July and August and hatch as caterpillars of " geometer " or " looper " class, having normal three pairs of proper legs just

Caterpillars of magpie moth are pest of gooseberries and currants. Aphis also cause trouble

◀ **Mr. MIDDLETON** says : *You can't do good work with bad tools.* ▶

behind the head, but only two pairs of " pro-legs " or " sucker-feet " towards rear of body. Therefore must walk by " looping " body, drawing back legs up to front ones, then pushing these forward, and so on. When disturbed, save themselves from falling by releasing a silken thread on which to swing. These caterpillars feed for time, then hibernate for winter in cracks and crannies, under dead leaves, stones, etc. Emerge in spring and begin to eat young foliage of gooseberries. Bad attacks completely defoliate bushes. Spray shrubs with derris wash after fruit has been picked.

MAIZE : (See *Corn.*)

MANURE : All materials added to soils to increase plant-food contents, whether of animal origin or chemical fertilizers. Plants are made up of or contain between 20 and 30 chemical elements. By growing plants in special solutions, it has been found that 13 of these elements are absolutely essential. Without any one of them growth is incomplete or stunted. Essentials are carbon, hydrogen, oxygen, nitrogen, sulphur, phosphorus, iron, potassium, sodium, calcium, magnesium, silica and chlorine. Carbon is obtained from the air, in the gas carbon dioxide. Remainder are absorbed through roots from the soil. Of these only three are normally in short supply in soil—nitrogen, phosphates and potassium—and fertilizers are designed to supply them. Animal manures supply all the foods. Use of fertilizers only so stimulates growth as to make unreasonable demands on soil's plant foods, and while the three main ones are supplied the remaining six become exhausted and crops begin to fail. Recently been discovered that other elements such as boron, zinc, manganese, etc.—so-called " trace " elements—are essential to plants though only in minutest traces. Animal manures also supply these, while use of fertilizers alone tends to exhaust them. These manures or organic materials, such as rotten compost-heap refuse, are essential to soils, while fertilizers are also valuable. Both should be used together. Animal manures increase the humus content of soil, which not only contains plant foods but alters physical structure of soil. (See *Cross-Fertilization ; Farmyard Manure ; Feeding ; Compost Heap ; Green Manuring.*)

MARCH MOTH : One of moths whose caterpillars feed on leaves of fruit trees. Females are wingless and must climb trees to lay eggs. This they do in March. Grubs hatch out, feed on leaves, drop to soil and turn into pupæ, remaining there until spring, when adults emerge. Best control is to trap females with greasebands on tree trunks. Another control is to spray with lead arsenate in spring.

MARROW : (See *Vegetable Marrow.*)

MEALY BUG : Pest of plants under glass, particularly vines. They are about 1/10th-in. long, with flattened, oval body and covered with mealy wax. Fumigation with hydrocyanic acid gas is good method of control, or paraffin can be applied to clusters of pest with camelhair brush.

MILDEW : Various fungus diseases visible on outside of plants. Two main classes are powdery mildews, chiefly superficial in growth and easy to control by dusting with sulphur ; and downy mildews, which, while easy to see, are more deep-seated in tissues of plants, and are harder to control. Flowers of sulphur or green sulphur are best materials to use for dusting.

MILLIPEDES : Soil pests feeding on underground parts of plants. Long in body, which is divided into segments, each segment having two pairs of legs, as opposed to the centipede's one pair. Differ from centipede in being sluggish of movement. Common in sour and acid soils, so liming helps to discourage them. Naphthalene worked into soil at 4 ozs. per square yard helps to drive them away. Superphosphate put into seed drills when sowing helps to protect seedlings.

MINT : Popular herb. Prepare good patch of soil and plant young shoots in spring. Propagation is by division

of the roots or by cuttings taken in summer and rooted in boxes. Plant will thrive in shady corner.

MITES : Group of animals closely allied to spiders and belonging to class *Arachnida*. Not true insects, as they have eight legs instead of six. They are minute, and many are bad plant pests, difficult to control, e.g., red spider mite, big bud mite. Lime-sulphur is frequently used as a control, and so is petroleum wash such as *Volck*.

MOSAIC DISEASES : (See *Virus Diseases*.)

MULCH : Covering of soil surface round a plant with manure, or other organic material such as grass mowings. Protects roots from fluctuating temperatures, and drying during drought.

MURIATE OF POTASH : Important potash salt containing 50 per cent. of potash. As muriate, contains certain amount of chlorine—an impurity which can give slight check to growth   Therefore sulphate of potash is normally preferred although dearer. Muriate is just as good, but should be applied well in advance of sowing seeds or setting out plants. Potash in any form is now exceedingly valuable and should be used with care.

MUSHROOM : Luxury crop in wartime. An empty shed or cellar can be used for mushrooms, or you can make bed outside. Best time to start bed is June or July. Then mushrooms appear when year is cooling, and are not troubled by maggots, as are those produced at height of summer. Good, fresh horse-manure is necessary. Long straw is shaken out and short manure is placed in heap to heat up. Should be sheltered from rain. Turn it two or three times to allow worst of heat to work off. After eight or nine days beds can be made. Under cover, beds are made flat, about 12/15-in. deep and pressed down firmly. Out of doors, beds are placed in protected position and built into heaps 4-ft. wide and 3-ft. high. Bed is then covered with straw. Temperature of heap should be checked by thermometer, and when you have falling

heat of 75°–80° F., it is ready for spawning. Bricks of spawn are broken into pieces and pushed into manure about 1½-in. deep. Watch bed for spawn beginning to run, and when you can see threads of fungus mycelium pushing through manure, place layer of rather poor soil over bed and pat down. Keep outside beds protected with straw. Where manure is not available, chopped straw can be used alone, treating with special substances to induce fermenting and necessary heating up. Treat in same way as manure. Beds can be made up at any time, but those in bearing during summer are more prone to be troubled by fly. **Pests :** Mushroom fly, larvæ of which burrow in buttons, devouring them.   To prevent flies entering huts, cover ventilators with fine muslin and see there are no leaks anywhere else. When one crop finished, fumigate with hydrocyanic acid gas, and again when new bed has been made up. Another pest is species of mite, and this, too, is controlled by fumigation.

MUSHROOM SPAWN : Specially prepared bricks of manure, dried and hardened, which contain threads of fungus which gives rise to mushrooms. Usually purchased in cartons. It is advisable to buy a " 100 per cent. pure culture," as you can rely on this to contain only the true mushroom. The bricks are broken into egg-sized pieces and inserted in heaps of manure.

MUSTARD : Easily grown salad usually combined with cress. Sow seeds at intervals of fortnight in greenhouse during winter, and outside in summer. Usually cut when 2/3-in. high. Mustard is also used as green manure crop. When combined with cress, cress should be sown three days earlier, as it takes rather longer to germinate and grow.

N

NECTARINE : Smooth-skinned form of peach (for which see p. 117). Culture is identical. Can be grown in greenhouse or outside on south-facing wall. **Varieties :** *Cardinal, Early Rivers, Lord Napier.*

NEMATODES : (See *Eelworms*.)

NETTLE-LEAF DISEASE : (See *Reversion*.)

NICOTINE : Effective insecticide. Alkaloid extracted from tobacco waste, and normally purchased at 98 per cent. strength. Diluted with water and mixed with soft soap or other spreader to make effective spray. Suggested recipe is nicotine, 1 fluid oz ; potash soft soap, 1 lb. ; water 10 gallons.

NITRATE OF AMMONIA : Nitrogenous fertilizer containing 35 per cent. nitrogen. Normally too strong for ordinary use, but often employed to mix in general fertilizers.

NITRATE OF LIME : Nitrates are very soluble and quickly available to plants. This one contains 13 per cent. nitrogen and also lime, which makes it suitable for adding to heavy soils. Has disadvantage of being deliquescent, or absorbing moisture so rapidly that it melts. Consequently should be purchased in wooden casks. Usual application is ½ oz. to square yard.

NITRATE OF POTASH : Saltpetre. Excellent fertilizer for producing quick growth. Contains about 17 per cent. nitrogen. Usual dressing is ½/1 oz. per square yard, or used as liquid manure dissolve ½ oz. in 1 gallon of water.

NITRATE OF SODA : Most commonly used of nitrates. Also called Chile saltpetre or nitre. Contains 15½ per cent. nitrogen, and quantities used are same as nitrate of potash. These nitrates are purely ·stimulants, and greatest value is to encourage growth of green crops.

NITRO-CHALK : Fertilizer of which nitrate of ammonia is basis. Excellent on heavy soils in place of sulphate of ammonia, which tends to make them more sticky. Usual application 1/1½ ozs. per square yard to growing plants, or just before sowing or planting.

NITROGEN : Essential element to plants. At least 4/5ths of the atmosphere is made up of nitrogen, yet this gas is not available to plants. They obtain it from soil in form of nitrates so far as is known. Only cases where atmospheric nitrogen is used is when nitrifying bacteria on roots of plants of pea family (*legumes*), fix it and hand it to plants in exchange for place to live and for food. Nitrogen has effect on plants of stimulating growth and developing leaf surface. Lack is shown in stunted growth and underdeveloped plants.

NYMPH : Larval stage of many insects, such as the apple sucker, greenhouse leaf-hopper, or cockroaches. Most insects have larvæ which in no way resemble adults (e.g., caterpillars of butterflies) ; but nymphs do resemble their adults, usually being small replicas, wingless or with rudimentary wings. They grow to adult size by moulting skins.

O

ONIONS : Difficult vegetable to grow really well, but average results obtained without much difficulty. Chief requirements are firm soil, rich soil, and plenty

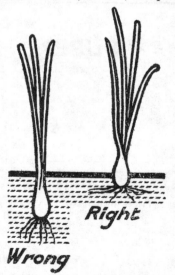

Right

Wrong

of sun at the season's end to help ripening. Onion can be worked into ordinary crop rotation and moved to different part of garden each year like other plants, or grown in the same place continuously if special onion bed is prepared and given preferential treatment in way of manure. Onion bed is first part of the garden to be dug in autumn. Early digging allows soil to settle. This is important, as onion does not flourish on loose, spongy soil. Also obtains maximum weathering. Dig as deeply as you can, the best method being bastard trenching (which see) two spits deep. This breaks up soil thoroughly to depth of 2 ft., and manure can be mixed in at different levels. Heavy soils should be ridged on top to expose large surface to weather. In spring, when soil is in good condition for working, give bed dressing of bone meal, wood ashes and old soot, and fork them into surface. Loosen soil few inches down and remove any large stones. Leave thus until ready for planting or sowing. Seeds of autumn-sown onions are put in during August. Sheltered position is chosen, and seed sown in drills 12-in. apart. Varieties used for this purpose are Italian or Tripoli onions, such as *Giant Rocca*, *Red and White Tripoli* and *Giant Zittau*. In south and midlands onions will normally overwinter successfully, but in north they will need protection. Better to sow in cold frame and only put lights on about December when weather begins to get bad. Alternatively, cloches can be used to cover rows, or temporary frame erected over them. Plant on to onion bed in March or as soon as weather permits. These onions should mature in July or August, but are prone to run to seed. When seed heads appear snap them off ; bulbs will be useful in any case. To obtain large onions, sow seeds in greenhouse in January of such varieties as *Premier*, *Ailsa Craig*, or *Cranston's Excelsior*. Put in boxes of good, well-mixed soil, and sow broadcast or space seeds 1-in. apart each way. Latter method obviates pricking out, but blanks are

likely where seeds fail to germinate, and can be filled from other boxes. After sowing, water boxes and cover with sheet of glass and paper until seeds have germinated. Keep in a temperature of 55–60° F. When seedlings are through, remove glass and paper and place boxes as near light as possible. Keep in greenhouse week or two before planting out, when they should be moved into frame and gradually hardened off. Plant out in April or soon as possible. Care needed in planting, particularly on heavier soils. Remove plants from boxes, few at a time, taking care not to damage roots. Make holes with trowel, put roots in, and firm with hands. In planting, depth should be no more than small bulb at the base of the plant. If put in deeper plants become thick-necked ; if shallower, apt to be blown about and find difficulty in getting hold. On light sandy soils plants can be put in more deeply, as sandy soil does not prevent bulbs from swelling. Heavier soils tend to cap, and by squeezing bulb make plants thick-necked. Distances apart 12 by 9 in. For ordinary crops, sow seed direct on to bed in March in rows 12-in. apart. Sow thinly. In many parts of north, sowing is often delayed until well into April ; hence it is better to raise plants inside and plant out. Those sown outside can either be thinned to one every six inches, or left unthinned. Latter method has advantage of not attracting fly. Smaller bulbs are produced, but yield per row is greater. These small bulbs keep well. Varieties for ordinary purposes : *James Keeping*, *Bedfordshire Champion*. All onions, autumn-sown or otherwise, should have occasional dressings of general fertilizer. Salad onions can be sown at any time during summer. Leave unthinned and pull as required.

ONION FLY : Similar pest to carrot fly. Widespread nuisance. Adult fly is grey, and resembles house fly in shape. Appear in spring and lay eggs on neck or small bulbs of onions and in soil nearby. Eggs are white and very small, hatch soon, usually after three days,

◀ Mr. MIDDLETON says : *Don't plant fruit trees too deeply.* ▶

and maggots make their way to base of onions and bore way in to feed. Attacked plants turn yellow and obviously look sick. If pulled up, fat, dirty-white maggots will be found inside. Control of pest is not easy, but following are a few things that can be done, particularly if you have had it before. Early planting helps, and is one of advantages of autumn-sown onions, as pest attacks smaller plants rather than larger ones. Application of deterrent is usual control. Chemicals are put down to keep off adult flies and prevent them laying eggs. Naphthalene, paraffin and sand, and paraffin emulsion are in this category, while old soot dusted on frequently has beneficial effect. Naphthalene should be hoed in at side of rows. Calomel dust applied to base of plants has lately been used with effect ; eggs laid in it are killed.

ONION MILDEW : Fungus disease which commonly attacks onions, generally bad in wet seasons. Disease starts on leaves which turn yellow and decay ; spreads to bulbs which go soft and rot. Where trouble has arisen, change location of onion bed, and choose sunny, well-drained spot. Dust plants with flowers of sulphur.

ONION SETS : Where ordinary onion culture is not easy, " sets " are sometimes used instead of plants. They are small bulbs about size of marble, raised from seed sown late previous year. Formerly many were imported from Middle East. If too large they tend to bolt ; if too small they merely produce leaves and no bulbs. Sets are planted in March, being pushed half into soil 6-in. apart in rows 1-ft. apart.

ORGANIC MANURES : Organic, used in this sense, means produced from living material, or material which has lived, as distinct from minerals. Manures are usually divided into natural, such as farmyard manure, and artificial. Artificial is again divided into two classes : organic, such as bone meal, and dried blood, both animal products ; and inorganic, such as sulphate of ammonia and nitrate of soda, both pure chemicals. Organic fertilizer is preferable to inorganic fertilizer.

OYSTER SHELL SCALE : Scale insect, shaped rather like oyster shell, which is pest of plums, apple, pear, apricot, peach and nectarine trees. Occurs in large numbers on bark, and trees are greatly weakened. Difficult to control. Badly-infected trees should be cut down and burned.

P

PARAFFIN EMULSION : Effective insecticide, particularly useful to keep insects such as flies from laying eggs in or near plants. Smell seems to make plants distasteful. The ingredients are 1 pint paraffin, $\frac{1}{4}$ lb. soft soap, 10 gallons water. To make, boil some of water and dissolve soft soap in it. Keep stirring, pour in paraffin, and make up to 10 gallons with water. Place syringe in liquid, and work forcibly to get thorough mixing of ingredients. Apply to celery, carrots, onions, and other plants attacked by flies.

PARIS GREEN (*Arsenic oxide*): Strong poison, must be used with care. Commonly used and mixed with bait, such as bran, to kill pests like cockroaches, earwigs and slugs.

PARSLEY : Herb much used for garnishing and flavouring. Two sowings are usual, in April and July, to provide succession through most of year. Seed is rather slow in germinating, so some should be sown in boxes in greenhouse in March, planting out in April. Those sown outside should be thinned to 6-in. apart. Favourite position for parsley is along side of path as edging.

PARSNIP : Easily-grown root vegetable. Thrives best on land manured year before for some other crop, and deeply dug. Sow in February or March, the sooner the better. Mark out drills 15/18-in. apart, and put in pinches of seed at intervals of 9-in. Sow little radish seed in drill. This will germinate before parsnip and indicate rows, so that hoeing can be done. Remove the radishes when ready and thin out parsnips to one at each station. No

◀ **Mr. MIDDLETON says :** *I like to see a nice row of peas*

special treatment is required apart from weeding and dressing of general fertilizer. On hard, heavy soils, bore holes 2-ft. deep with bar, and fill with fine soil. Sow few seeds at top of each. This is laborious but worth while when growing for exhibition. Few troubles affect parsnips : the worst is rust, which occurs on the roots. This is not a disease, but is due to rupturing of skin cells in sudden growth after dry weather. Fungi enter cells and cause brown rust-like appearance. Parsnips can be left in garden all winter. Lift as required.

Varieties : *Student, Hollow Crown, Offenham.*

PEA : Popular summer vegetable. Main sowings are from March to August (in north, April to July). In favoured districts, seeds can be sown in November on warm border, but this is too risky for general use. Land should be deeply dug and mixed with farmyard manure. Dressing of bone meal, about ¼ lb. per square yard, is worth while before sowing. Distance between rows is usually equal to height of variety. For earliest sowing choose dwarf, round-seeded variety. Take out drill 9-in. wide and 3-in. deep, and scatter seeds along it 3-in. apart. When seedlings are through, protect from bird attacks by covering rows with black cotton. Stake with pea sticks (though this is not essential with dwarf varieties) or support with strong string netting. Taller varieties must be staked. To keep up continuous supply, sow seeds at fortnightly intervals. For successful culture of tall varieties, best method is to dig out a trench 10/12-in. deep in late winter, and to leave it open for some weeks to weather. Put in layer of manure, fill with soil, and sow seeds. Feed with liquid manure as they grow.

Varieties : *DWARF—Little Marvel* (2 ft.), *Kelvedon Wonder* (2 ft.) ; *MEDIUM HEIGHT—Admiral Beatty* (3 ft.), *Senator* (3 ft.) ; *TALL—Gladstone* (4 ft.), *Autocrat* (5 ft.), *V.C.* (6 ft.).

PEACH : Grown in glasshouses or outdoors on wall facing south, usually fan-trained. Border should be well pre-pared, and ample quantity of ½-in. bones mixed with it before planting. Plant early autumn, allowing 12/15 ft. between trees. Train earliest branches sideways, gradually building up trees as years pass, working from outside and filling centre last. Pruning consists of cutting out wood which has borne fruit after fruit has been picked. Walls are brushed down, and branches and twigs tied in, evenly spaced out. Crossing of twigs should be avoided. In spring far too many shoots are produced, and should be thinned out. Fruits also need thinning before they " stone," reducing them to one per square foot. Culture consists of watering when necessary, feeding with fertilizer and occasionally with lime. Protect ripening fruit from birds, wasps and earwigs.

Varieties : *Duke of York, Royal George, Peregrine.*

PEACH LEAF-CURL : Disease of peaches and nectarines which causes malformation of the leaves. Spray with Bordeaux mixture in February or March, just before buds begin to swell.

PEAR : Popular fruit, easy to grow either in open or against wall. Plant healthy young trees in November, first preparing land well. Standard trees are planted 20-ft. apart, bush trees 10/12-ft., espalier trees on walls, 12 ft. Established pears are pruned in winter, leaders being tipped and laterals cut back to two or three buds. Summer pruning, especially of wall fruit, is important.

Good varieties : *William's Bon Chretien, Marie Louise, Doyenne de Comice, Winter Nelis, Conference.*

PERENNIAL : Plant which lives for more than two years, flowering and producing seed at regular intervals.

PERMANGANATE OF POTASH : Chemical substance consisting of purple-coloured crystals. Not used so much now as formerly in garden. Solution watered on soil destroys spores of fungi.

PERPETUAL SPINACH : (See *Spinach-Beet.*)

PESTS : The more important of these are dealt with separately. Garden pests range from mammals, such as moles, to tiny mites and insects. (See *Ammonia, Ant, Aphis, Apple Blossom Weevil, Apple Sawfly, Bean Aphis, Beet and Mangold Fly, Big Bud, Cabbage Aphis, Cabbage Caterpillars, Cabbage Root Fly, Cabbage White Fly, Capsid Bugs, Carrot Fly, Celery Fly, Click Beetle, Cockchafer, Cockroach, Codlin Moth, Colorado Beetle, Crane Fly, Cut-worms, Earwig, Eelworms, Leatherjackets, Loganberry Beetle, Magpie Moth, March Moth, Mealy Bug, Millipedes, Mites, Moth, Onion Fly, Oyster Shell Scale, Red Spider Mite, Repellants, Scale Insects, Slugs and Snails, Sterilization, Thrips, Weevil, White Fly, Winter Moths, Wireworms, Woodlice, Woolly Aphis.*

PISTIL : Female parts of flower containing the stigma, style and ovary.

PLANTING : Vegetable plants are usually set in holes made with a trowel or a dibber. Soil is firmed around roots. Seed potatoes are best planted in drill taken out with spade or drag hoe. Never plant when soil is wet and sticky. Often necessary on heavy soils to walk on plank while planting. Planting of fruit trees and bushes needs special care. Land should be dug correctly first, because holes made in undug land may become collecting centres for water. Take out hole at least 2-ft. across, and remove all top soil. Fork the subsoil and work in little manure. Sprinkle soil over this, drive in stake, and put in tree or bush. Cut damaged roots and spread others evenly. See that depth of planting is about same as plant has been in before ; soil mark can be seen on stem. Cover roots with soil and, before firming, work plant gently up and down to settle soil around roots. Tread firmly and finish surface with layer of loose soil.

PLUM : Can be grown on walls or in open garden. Against walls plant 10/12-ft. apart ; in open, 12/20-ft. apart, according to size of tree. Plums can be planted against an east, west or south wall.

Varieties : *Early Laxton, Early Transparent Gage, Dennison's Superb, Coe's*

Golden Drop (Dessert), *Czar, Belle de Louvain, Victoria* (Culinary).

Pests : *Plum Leaf-Curling Aphis*, for which winter spraying is a control.

Disease : *Silver Leaf* (for which see p. 123). Branches affected by this should be cut out and burned·before mid-July.

POLE : Rod or Perch. 30¼ square yards.

POLLEN : Yellow dust produced on the anthers of flowers. Consists of male half-cells or gametes. Essential for proper fruit and seed production that it be carried to pistil or female organs. For instance, fruits of tomatoes will not develop correctly unless flowers have been properly pollinated.

PORTUGAL CABBAGE, or *Couve Tronchuda* : Vegetable grown for the thick white midribs of leaves. Similar cultivation to ordinary cabbage.

POTASH or **POTASSIUM :** Essential food element for plants, contained in various fertilizers such as sulphate of potash and muriate of potash. Also present in wood ashes and flue dust.

POTATO : Order seed potatoes early, and set up in boxes to sprout. This advances growth, permits diseased tubers to be picked out, and number of sprouts to be reduced to two per tuber. Large seeds can be cut into halves, each portion to have two sprouts or eyes. Ideal crop for planting on newly-broken land. Plant earlies end of March or early April, according to locality. Distance apart 2 ft. by 15 in. Follow with second-earlies and maincrop, 2 ft. 6 in. by 18 in. Plant in drills 5/6-in. deep. As plants grow, earth them up, especially on dirty land, as it helps to clean. Give at least one dressing of general fertilizer immediately before ridging. Watch for blight attacks, and spray with Bordeaux mixture as preventative or control. Lift earlies in July and August, following on with others. Maincrops should be lifted and stored in sacks or clamps.

Varieties : *EARLIES—Sharpe's Express, Arran Pilot, Di Vernon : SECOND EARLIES—Great Scot, Arran Banner.*

◀ **Mr. MIDDLETON** says : *You'll get a heavier crop of larger*

Maincrop : *Kerr's Pink, Majestic, Golden Wonder.*

Pests : *Slugs, Wireworms, Capsid Bugs, Greenfly, Eelworms.*

Diseases : *Scab, Black Leg, Blight, Dry Rot, Mosaic* and *Leaf Roll.*

POTATO BLIGHT : Common disease. Farmers now spray crops regularly as a routine measure whether disease is present or not. Usually appears in south in early June, and as year proceeds goes further north. Disease does not usually occur where there is sulphur in atmosphere as in towns. First attacks are usually on lower leaves, but later it reaches upper parts of plant. Dark green spots appear on leaves, which turn brown or black. White mould-like growth can usually be seen around margins of patches, caused by spore-bearing bodies of fungus. These spots spread infection. Spraying or dusting with Bordeaux mixture is usual remedy. Dust can be purchased already made up. Spray should consist of bluestone (copper sulphate), 4 ozs., hydrated lime, 5 ozs., water, $2\frac{1}{2}$ gallons. Bluestone is dissolved in quart of water, and lime mixed with remainder. When bluestone is completely dissolved, pour it into lime-water and stir well. Tubers may be infected with disease. These should never be stored, but picked out and only clean ones put into clamp. When crop is infected with blight, cut off tops at least week before lifting, and burn.

PRICKING-OUT : When seedlings are set out few inches apart in boxes, frames, or outside beds, to grow on for transplanting, they are " pricked out." Term probably comes from use of small dibber to prick holes in soil.

PRUNING : Pruning of fruit trees and bushes is, first, to train them and produce a particular form of tree. Afterwards aims are to space out branches and give them room for development, to encourage production of fruits, and to remove any dead or diseased wood. Summer pruning of fruit trees is done to ripen wood and

expose fruit to sun. Winter pruning is begun soon after leaf fall and completed by January. Apples and pears which bear fruit on short spurs are carefully pruned according to each tree's requirements. Side shoots are cut back to two buds, and main leader by third of its length. Other trees and bushes are pruned according to how they carry their fruits. The raspberry, for instance, bears fruit mainly on young canes, so each year after fruiting old canes are cut out. Blackcurrants carry fruit on old wood, so they are only thinned out, an old branch being removed each year as a rule. All pruning cuts should be clean, and large ones should be painted to exclude disease spores.

PUDDLING : It is common practice when planting out in dry weather to

potatoes from two shoots, or even one, than from half a dozen. ▶

make thick mixture of clay and water and squeeze some around roots of plants, or just to dip them in it. With brassicas, lime is frequently mixed with puddle, and this helps to ward off clubroot.

Q

QUASSIA : Insecticide formerly used much more than to-day. Can be bought as Quassia Extract, or " chips " can be obtained and steeped in water to provide solution. Soft-bodied insects such as greenfly are vulnerable to it. Said to stop birds pecking leaves if sprayed on ground near pea plants.

QUICKLIME : (See *Lime*.)

QUINCE : Tree grown for decoration and fruit. Fruit is hard, but has various culinary uses, such as flavouring and preserving, and for making jellies and marmalade.

R

RADISH : Popular salad, easy to grow, with different types of roots of many colours. Small-rooted types may be round, such as *French Breakfast* or *Turnip-Rooted* varieties ; or .oval, or elongated. Colours vary from white to scarlet. Long-rooted varieties can achieve foot in length, such as the white one, *White Icicle*, or the pink one, *China Rose*. Sowings of small forms may be made at fortnightly intervals in open garden throughout summer from April. Sow thinly in shallow drills ; if too thick, do not swell. May be grown as intercrop between rows of larger plants. During winter may be raised in greenhouse or frame or over hot-beds. Larger varieties may be sown in June and July and thinned to 4/6-in. apart. Lift in September or October and store in sand.

RASPBERRY : Cultivation of raspberry is simple. Thrives in most soils, but prefers good strong loam. Thorough digging is essential, and manure should be worked in. Sheltered but open sunny position is best site. Obtain good healthy young canes, free from virus disease. Plant in November, if possible, 2-ft. apart, in rows 4/5-it. apart,

running north to south. In spring, before growth starts, cut canes back to within 10/12 in. of ground, to encourage production of fruiting canes from base. Do not try to get fruit first year by leaving cane uncut ; it will only spoil future development. Provide support by inserting 4-ft. posts 10 12-ft. apart along rows. Run two strands of wire from post to post, one at top, the other halfway down, and tie growths to them. Subsequent cultivation consists of gentle forking round plants in spring and dressing of general fertilizer. In winter, mulch of manure is advisable. Protect fruit from birds and, after it has been picked, cut out fruiting canes and tie in young ones. Autumn fruiting raspberries are cut down to ground in spring.

Varieties : *Pyne's Royal, Reward, Norfolk Giant,* with *Lloyd George* either as summer or autumn fruiting variety.

Pests : *Aphids, Raspberry Beetle* and *Raspberry Sawfly.*
The worst diseases are of virus type, such as *Raspberry Mosaic.*

RED CABBAGE : Cultivation is same as ordinary cabbage.

RED CURRANTS : Propagated by cuttings of young, ripened wood in September. Take 10/12-in. long, and remove all buds except top five. Insert 9-in. apart in drills in open garden. Removing bottom buds causes plant to grow on single main stem called a leg. Plants can be grown as bushes or trained as cordons on wall. Plant bushes 4/5-ft. apart in early winter, and later cut back main stems to half length. Future pruning aims at keeping centre of bush open and encouragement of fruiting. Prune after leaf fall, cut back all lateral growths to two buds, and just tip leaders. Where birds may peck buds, leave pruning until spring. Feed each year with complete fertilizer and give a mulch of animal manure.

Varieties : *Fay's Prolific, Laxton's No. 1, Raby Castle.*

Main Pests : *Greenfly* and *Big Bud Mite.* Latter is rarely so bad as on blackcurrants.

◄ **Mr. MIDDLETON says :** *Plants are cleverer than*

RED LEAD : Red powder used to dust on pea and bean seeds to discourage mice and birds from digging them up. First damp with paraffin.

RED SPIDER MITE : Tiny creatures belonging to spider group, having eight legs. Greenhouse red spider mite is best known as common in glasshouses, particularly where conditions are dry and hot. Also number of species which are pests of fruit trees, and can be controlled by killing the eggs laid on bark of trees. Ordinary tar-distillate wash is not satisfactory, but good petroleum spray or D.N.C. is reasonably effective. Tar-distillate spraying may be actually followed by an increase in number of mites as insects which prey on them and keep them in check are probably killed. Greenhouse form can be kept in check by good cultural methods such as adequate ventilation and keeping moist atmosphere by damping down, and by syringing plants with water daily. Fruit trees inside can be sprayed with lime-sulphur 1 in 30, just before blossoms open. Liver of sulphur can also be used as spray. In some glasshouses, as where cucumbers are being grown, naphthalene may be vapourised. In tomato houses, straw can be put down in July and swept up in October. Stalks provide ideal places for mites to hibernate. Thus many can be destroyed.

REPELLENTS (*Deterrents*) : Use of chemicals to prevent pests attacking particular plants, e.g., spraying celery with paraffin emulsion to keep fly away. Following can be used : naphthalene, paraffin and sand, paraffin emulsion, soot and lime mixed, dichlorobenzene.

REVERSION : Disease of blackcurrant bushes, cause is not completely known. It is virus disease, noticeable for alterations in shape of leaves, which slowly lose distinctive currant form and become like nettle leaves. Therefore also called nettle-leaf disease. Flower bunches are affected and do not fruit well. Trouble is progressive and whole bush may revert. Destroy badly-affected bushes.

RHUBARB : Easily-grown vegetable used as fruit. Buy good, strong crowns which have not been forced. Roots which have been forced are frequently placed on market for sale, and take few years to become useful. Plants can also be raised from seeds which can be sown in boxes or outside in April. Thin to 12-in. apart, and transplant to permanent position following spring. Plant in February or March 4-ft. apart, just covering tops with soil. Cover with animal manure. Do not pick any stalks first year, and remove flower heads which form. Old crowns can be divided in spring to increase quantity. Stalks can be obtained from November on by forcing. Earliest are forced under cover in warm shed or greenhouse. Lift good roots and leave on surface of soil, exposed to weather for 10 days or so. Take inside, place under bench, and pack with soil. Water thoroughly and exclude light. Forcing outside takes bit longer. Place deep boxes or barrels over selected crowns and cover with layer of fresh manure or dry leaves.

RIDGING : Throwing up soil into ridges while digging exposes larger surface to beneficial action of weather. Heavy soils are better if ridged, as they need maximum weathering. Divide garden into strips 3-ft. wide. Take out trench 1-ft. wide across end of first strip. Clean out crumbs and put soil on path. Turn over soil into trench, as when digging ordinarily, but do it in the following manner : Cut out one spadeful 1-ft. wide and 1-ft. deep, and place near centre of trench. Cut out next spadeful and place it beside first, also near centre. Cut out third and last spadeful and place it on top of other two. Clean out crumbs and put on top. Work backwards in this way, up and down various strips, and thus create series of ridges.

ROOD : Quarter of acre.

ROOT PRUNING : Method of checking fruit trees which produce too much growth and too little fruit. Take out trench 2/3-ft. from stem, about 1-ft. wide and as deep as necessary. Cut back all strong roots, but not fibrous ones. Refill with soil. Do work in early winter. Trench can be taken all round tree, or halfway one year and other half next year. Rather laborious job which has to some extent been superseded by bark ringing.

ROTATION OF CROPS : Crops are normally classified for garden purposes into four groups : (1) Permanent crops like rhubarb, asparagus, seakale, fruit trees and bushes, which occupy land for many years and do not enter into ordinary rotation ; (2) green crops like cabbage, sprouts, kales, etc., and, perhaps, leeks ; (3) potato and root crops, including turnips, carrots, beet and onions ; (4) pea and bean crops. Last three groups are important in rotation. Gardener should try to organise three groups of roughly equal size, and to do it some little adjustment may be necessary between groups. For instance, it may be advisable to add onions to pea and bean class. Any alteration should take into consideration requirements of respective vegetables. As an example, study Cropping Plan on pages 50-51. Groups, being of equal size, can be interchanged each year; and location of each should be altered so that it comes back to same position once in three years. Advantages of rotation are that it evens out demands on plant foods in soil, and spreads effects of various plants over all the garden. For example, roots of parsnips and carrots have penetrating power and help to break up soil ; intensive cultivation received by potatoes, and possibilities of pest and disease attacks are lessened. Strawberries, if grown, must be included in rotation.

RUNNER BEAN : (See *Bean*.)

RUSTS : Class of fungi, parasitic on green plants. General symptom is brown discoloration caused by production of spores which resemble rust. Wheat rust is probably most important.

S

SAGE : Popular herb which grows as small shrubby plant. Thrives best in light, well-drained soil. Raised from seeds or cuttings. Take cuttings of soft young growths in May and June, insert in boxes of sandy soil, and put in frame or under cloches. Cut growths in August and September and dry slowly.

SALSIFY : Also called Vegetable Oyster. Grown for roots. Sow in drills 12-in. apart and ½-in. deep. Thin seedlings to 9-in. apart. Hoe and weed in summer, and apply dressing of general fertilizer. When leaves change colour in autumn, lift and store roots in sand.

SALTPETRE : (See *Nitrate of Potash*.)

SAVORY (*Satureia*) : There are two forms of this useful herb, Summer Savory and Winter Savory. First is sown during April in drills 12-in. apart and thinned to 6-in. Pull up plants in autumn and hang up to dry. Winter savory is sown about same time on seed bed, and seedlings are transplanted when few inches high to 15-in. apart. Savories are bushes, and plants will last for a few years. Young growths are cut and dried.

SAVOY CABBAGE : Hardy form of cabbage grown for winter use. Sow in April on seed bed and transplant to permanent positions during May and June. Plant 2-ft. by 2-ft. Varieties for succession are *Best of All*, *Ormskirk Early*, *Ormskirk Medium*, *Ormskirk Late*, and *Rearguard*. Tiny varieties, such as *Early Ulm*, which mature in September and October, should be planted 18 in. by 18 in.

SCAB DISEASE : Disease of apple and pear. Causes blotching and cracking of fruits. Spray with lime-sulphur or Bordeaux mixture at least three times : (1) in " green-bud " stage ; (2) in " pink-bud " stage ; (3) in " petal-fall " stage.

SCALE INSECTS : Group of insects found on plants out of doors and in greenhouse. Young scales hatch from eggs, crawl to young thin-skinned parts of plants, push proboscis into plant and settle down, staying there for remainder

◄ Mr. MIDDLETON **says :** *An enormous amount of good stuff is*

of life. These are all females ; males are tiny winged-creatures.

SCARLET RUNNER : (See *Bean, Runner*.)

SCORZONERA : Root vegetable ; also called Viper's Grass. Similar in cultivation to salsify.

SEAKALE : Hardy vegetable grown for blanched shoots which are forced. Likes rich, well-dug soil. Propagated from pieces of thick root, known as thongs. Thongs are taken from crowns lifted for forcing and stored in sand until required. Plant out thongs in March either 18-in. apart in rows 2-ft. apart, or in triangles 1-ft. apart with 3-ft. between triangles. Triangle method is adopted for outdoor forcing. Can be raised from seed sown on bed in April, thinned to 6-in. apart, and transplanted following February. To force, lift roots and place 2-in. apart in boxes of soil. Place under greenhouse bench in temperature of 50° F., and keep in dark. To force out of doors, cover with deep box or barrel and heap over with strawy manure or dry leaves.

SEAKALE BEET : Grown for thick white midribs of leaves. Cultivation is similar to Spinach Beet (see p. 124).

SEAWEED : Seaweed can be used to make a valuable manure. Collect and build into compost heaps.

SEEDS : (See page 130.)

SETS : Portion of plant for putting out in soil. Usually applied to portions of roots or tubers.

SHALLOT : Species of allium resembling small onion. Can be raised from seeds, but is usually propagated from cloves. Plant in February, pushing them half into the soil, 9 in. by 12 in., and not burying them. Many growths will be produced, and base of each growth will swell into small bulb. Keep hoed and weed-free, and give dressing of fertilizer. In July, leaves will die down, and plants can be lifted, ripened and stored.

SILVER LEAF : Serious disease of plum trees, which also attacks apples, pears and peaches, nectarines, some bush fruits, and ornamental trees such as laburnum. Leaves of affected branches become silver-grey. Fungus causing disease enters through cuts or wounds and spreads through stem. Affected branches should be cut out before middle of July. Begin high up branch and cut pieces off until brown stain in tissues of wood has disappeared. Burn prunings.

SLUGS and SNAILS : Familiar to everyone. Slugs are more widespread. Snails, and larger forms of slugs, can be reduced considerably by trapping. They hide during day, and traps such as boards, pots, cut potatoes, etc., can be put down in strategic positions for them to hide under. Examine daily and destroy pests. A mixture of Paris green and bran, Meta and bran, or Meta and dried tea-leaves, can be used as poison bait, placed in small heaps among crops. These baits are not very effective against small black slugs which feed underground as well as on the surface—those which eat roots and bore holes in potatoes. A liquid slug destroyer watered on the soil, preferably at night, is best for these. Quicklime or salt dusted on soil at night when slugs are about are useful. Old remedy of hand-picking is still as good as any. Get a long hatpin, a tin of strong salt water, and a lamp, and search for them at night, spearing into salt water.

SOOT : Can be used to feed plants, as it contains little nitrogen, and also as insecticide. Do not use soot fresh : it contains harmful sulphur, and should be kept in an open shed for six months.

SPINACH : Two forms of ordinary spinach are grown, Round-seeded in summer, and Prickly-seeded in winter. First sowings of round are made in March, and at regular intervals until June. Can be grown as intercrop. As later sowings tend to run to seed in dry weather, use varieties such as *Longstanding Round*. Thin to 4/6 in. between the plants. Sow prickly or winter spinach in August or early September in rows 12 in. apart, and thin to 6 in.

wasted every autumn, because it's not properly harvested and stored. ▶

SPINACH BEET : Perpetual spinach. Beet grown for strong green leaves. Two sowings usually made, first in April for summer crop, the second in July for winter. Sow in drills 15-in. apart and thin seedlings to 9 in. Hoe, and give dressing of general fertilizer. When cutting, remove leaves from several plants instead of cutting one plant right down.

SPINACH, NEW ZEALAND : Grown for tips of shoots. Requires ample room. Sow in May in pinches, or in pots under glass in April for planting out in May. Plants should be 3-ft. apart.

SPIT : Spade's depth of soil.

SPRAYS : Numerous chemicals are used to spray plants for control of insect pests and diseases. Applied with syringe or large sprayers such as pneumatic knapsack type. When your stirrup-pump is demobilised from war duty, it will serve well for most garden spraying jobs.

SPUR : Short, fruit-bearing growth on fruit trees.

STANDARD : Fruit tree grown on clean stem 6 ft. from ground.

STERILISATION OF SOIL : To kill fungi and pests, soil can be partially sterilised by heating or by treating with chemicals. Most efficient method is steaming which, however, requires fairly large apparatus for any considerable quantity of soil. Temperature is raised to 190° F. and maintained for 10 minutes. This is sufficient to destroy most pests. Baking can also be done, and small quantities can be heated over a fire. Danger with this method is complete burning out of soil. Chemicals are not so effective as steaming, but are often only method possible in small garden. Formalin and cresylic acid are two chemicals used, and there are several proprietary liquids on market.

STOPPING : When plant has reached adequate size, it is stopped, that is, growing point is pinched out. Stopping is also used to make plants bush out.

STORAGE OF VEGETABLES : Main-crops of root vegetables, such as potatoes, carrots, turnips, beet, etc., are harvested in late September and October. Small quantities can be placed in sacks and kept in cool shed or room for early use. Large numbers require more elaborate treatment. Commonest method of storing out of doors is to build a clamp. All root crops keep excellently in these. Carrots, beet, turnips, salsify, kohl rabi, etc., keep well in sand. Remove leaves and growths and arrange roots in layers, putting sand over each layer. They may be put in large boxes or barrels, or heap can be built in a corner of shed. Alternatively a place can be made for them against outside wall by putting plank or two some 2 ft. from wall, making firm with supports. Put roots down in layers between wall and plank and cover with sand. See that drips do not fall from building on to store. In bad weather sacks can be placed over top. Crops such as parsnips, Jerusalem artichokes, and leeks may be left in open garden, as hardest weather will not harm them. Normally lifted and stored only when land is wanted for digging, or if prolonged spell of frost threatens which will prevent the crops being got for use as required. (See *Clamp*.)

STRAWBERRIES : Grown as rotational crop, beds being removed after third year. New bed is laid down each year to replace old one. Propagation is by layering runners produced by plants. Peg them into soils or into small pots. Remove when rooted. New beds are prepared by deep digging and adequate manuring. Set plants out 18 in. by 2 ft. Make firm, but do not bury crown. Planting can be done any time during winter, but if put in later than August, plants should not be allowed to fruit first year. Weed and hoe between growing plants. Give dressing of general fertilizer. When flowers are produced, put clean straw around plants on which fruits can rest. As soon as fruit shows, cover beds with small-mesh nets to keep out birds. Allow runners on one-year-old plants to develop for propagat-

ing, but remove all unnecessary runners. After picking fruits remove nets, straw, dead leaves, and weeds, and clean beds. **Varieties :** *Royal Sovereign, Tardive de Leopold, Sir Joseph Paxton.*
Pests : *Eelworm, Aphis, Ground Beetles, Strawberry Weevil, Slugs* and *Snails.*
Diseases : Virus diseases such as *Red Plant* and *Yellow Edge, Leaf Scorch, Leaf Spot.*

SUCKER : Growths from rootstock of plant as with raspberries. With grafted plants, such as apples, suckers should be removed.

SULPHATE OF AMMONIA : Nitrogenous fertilizer containing 20 per cent. nitrogen. Normally acid, though neutral form can be obtained. On heavy sour soils better to use nitro-chalk.

SULPHATE OF POTASH : Valuable and now scarce, potash fertilizer. Contains 48 per cent. potassium.

SULPHUR : Used in various forms as fungicide and insecticide. For use as dust, flowers of sulphur, green sulphur, or black sulphur, can be obtained. As fumigant, it can be vaporised or sulphur candles burned. For insects, used chiefly in form of lime-sulphur.

SULPHURIC ACID : Used as weed-killer chiefly among plants with straight, parallel-veined leaves.

SUPERPHOSPHATE OF LIME : Phosphatic fertilizer containing different proportion of phosphorus according to sample. The name, however, is somewhat misleading, as it contains no free lime.

SURFACE SOIL : Top 9 in. of soil is surface soil. Generally quite distinct from subsoil below, and clear line of demarcation can often be seen.

SWEDE TURNIP : Large roots grown mainly for storage. Sow in May in rows 18-in. apart, and thin seedlings to 9 in. Hoe and weed, and give dressing of general fertilizer. Lift in autumn and store in small clamp.

T

TAP ROOT : Main central root of a plant, such as that of carrot or parsnip.

TAR-DISTILLATE WASHES : Spray fluids applied to fruit trees and shrubs in dormant season to kill insects and their eggs.

TETRACHLORETHANE : Liquid which rapidly vaporises. Used as fumigant to kill white flies in greenhouses.

THONG : Pieces of root used for cuttings, as with seakale and horseradish.

THRIPS : Minute black insects, pests of plants in open and indoors. Cause mottling of leaves, and plants lose vigour and look sick. Regular damping down discourages, but where prevalent spray with nicotine and soft soap solution.

TIGER BEETLES : Green beetles found in south and midlands, chiefly on light soils. They are beneficial.

TIP-LAYERING : (See *Layering*.)

TOADS : Very beneficial creatures, as they feed on slugs, snails, and other pests.

TOMATO : Valuable fruit grown either indoors or out. Most greenhouses can be used for cultivation. Tomatoes can be grown in boxes or pots, or troughs can be made up on greenhouse benches. Where no benches available, can be grown in ground. Soil should be well dug, incorporating manure or straw, and adding lime. Thoroughly soak a week or 10 days before planting to make sure subsoil is not dry. Soil to be imported should be thoroughly mixed of rough loam, sand, leaf-mould, a little old manure, and some bone meal. Raise plants by sowing seeds in boxes.

Nine Rules for Successful Fruit Bottling

BOTH methods of fruit bottling involve these points : (1) Use fresh fruit, thoroughly cleaned. (2) Get bottles with screw-bands or clip-tops, and with good rubber rings to exclude air. (3) Wash bottles and drain thoroughly.

I. Sterilising in Water

Probably this is the better method, but it demands a big vessel, such as a washing-boiler or a fish kettle. (1) Fill one-third of bottle with fruit, firmly packed but not crushed, then just cover fruit with cold water or syrup. Next fill another third, and finally the last one-third similarly, so that bottle is full to brim. (2) Get rid of air bubbles by turning the bottle from side to side. (3) Place rubber band and lid on bottle, and fix in place. (4) Place bottles in vessel, standing on wood. (5) Pour in cold water until bottles are completely covered. (6) Heat very slowly until temperature reaches 165° F., and maintain that temperature for ten minutes.

II. Sterilising in Oven

This method is perfectly efficient. (1) Fill bottle with fruit, firmly packed but not crushed, but do not add liquid. (2) Put lid and ring on bottle, but do not clamp down. (3) Place sheet of asbestos on oven shelf to avoid risk of bottles cracking. (4) Heat oven to about 250° F., then put in bottles and leave until fruit is cooked thoroughly (about 45 minutes). (5) Remove bottles and fill up with boiling syrup or boiling water. (6) Replace lids at once and seal with clips.

Testing Results

When the bottle is cool, remove clips, and see if lid is held by suction from inside bottle. If so, all is well. If not, there is a leak which must be sealed, and it will be necessary to re-sterilise.

Syrup

If you can afford sugar to make syrup, add four pounds of sugar to one gallon of water. Dissolve sugar, boil, and strain through butter-muslin.

◀ Mr. MIDDLETON says : *Every plant has its enemies.* ▶

Space them out 2/3-in. apart to save pricking out, and keep in temperature of 60° F. When 2/3-in. high, pot into 3½-in. pots. Plant when 10/12-in. tall, 15 in. by 2 ft., and when soil is warm. Grown on benches, watering needs careful attention. In borders, should not be watered until first truss has set. Assist pollination of flowers by spraying plants daily at noon with water. Give plants support as they grow, tying to stakes, wires or strings. Top-dress occasionally and feed with fertilizers. Remove side shoots as produced. Stop plants when they have reached the top of house, usually after eight trusses are formed. When fruit is well formed, little of lower foliage can be removed to expose fruits. Varieties for indoor cultivation are *Ailsa Craig, Market King, Stonor's M.P., Best of All*, etc. Cultivation out of doors is not possible everywhere. In south and midlands, can be grown in open but sheltered position. In north, they are only possible grown against wall facing south. Raise from seeds sown in April and plant out in June, when danger of frost is passed. Stop after two leaves above third truss in the north; in south, four trusses may be allowed. Most indoor varieties are suitable for outdoor culture and on the whole seem to do better than special outdoor varieties. Fruits not ripened outdoors can be finished off in warm room.

Pests : *White Fly, Red Spider Mite, Tomato Eelworm, Tomato Moth.*

Diseases : *Tomato Leaf-Mould or Blight, Sleepy Disease, Tomato Stripe, Foot Rot, Damping Off, etc.*

TRUSS : Compact cluster of flowers or fruit.

TUBER : Botanical name for swollen underground stem such as a potato. Distinct from swollen roots, such as carrots, turnips, etc., which are also natural storage organs.

TURNIP : Easily-grown root crops. Sow from April to July in open garden, in drills 12-in. apart, and thin plants to 6-in. White six-week type matures early. Globe forms take a little longer,

and may be lifted and stored. Turnip tops are often used as winter green. For this purpose sow seeds from July to September according to district.

Varieties : *Golden Ball, Orange Jelly, Snowball, Chirk Castle, Manchester Market.*

Pests : *Flea Beetle, Sawfly, Aphis.*

Diseases : *Clubroot, Dry Rot, Soft Rot.*

TURNIP GALL WEEVIL : This pest causes swellings on roots of cabbages and related plants which closely resemble clubroot disease. Plants from nurseryman may have swellings on roots. If caused by clubroot, seller is breaking the law, but if due to gall weevil he is not. To test, cut a few lumps. If small grub inside or hole where one has been, then trouble is gall weevil. However, if no grub found, and root is solid white flesh, swellings are due to clubroot. Do not plant these, but you can plant those attacked by insect after cutting open any galls and destroying grubs. Turnip gall weevil adults are small beetle-like creatures which emerge from hibernation in spring and seek out suitable plants such as cabbages, turnips, swedes, Brussels sprouts, etc., in which to lay eggs in the skin of root. Larvæ hatch out and begin to feed on roots, tissue swelling out to produce galls. Control is not easy, but you must pull up all roots of used plants.

V

VEGETABLE MARROW : Bush form is suitable for cultivation in open garden, while trailing form is ideal for growing on soil heaps and shelters. Sow seeds indoors singly in small pots in April for planting out early June. Prepare site by taking out hole 18 in. to 2 ft. square and 1 ft. deep. Put in manure, fill with good soil and plant. Seeds may be sown out of doors, three to a position. Reduce to one later. Water with liquid manure occasionally as they grow. Stop long-trailing growths, to encourage production of side growths. Use when about foot long. When frost comes, marrows can be stored in dry room and will keep for months.

VEGETABLE OYSTER : (See *Salsify*.)

VIPER'S GRASS : (See *Scorzonera*.)

◀ **Mr. MIDDLETON** says : *Keep records and notes of successes*

VIRUS DISEASES : Form of disease caused by organisms or materials which have never yet been isolated. Sap from plants suffering from one of virus diseases can be injected into sap of healthy plant, and in short time latter will begin to show signs of infection, but it has not yet been found possible to discover causative material. Examples are leaf-roll of potato, stripe of tomatoes, the various mosaics of many plants, and crinkle and yellow edge of strawberries.

W

WASPS : Very beneficial in spring, as the queen wasps destroy many insects. Later they become pests as workers attack fruits. Trace to nests and destroy. Insert crystals of sodium cyanide and pour on to them hydrochloric acid to produce hydrocyanic-acid gas. Calcium cyanide purchased as a powder can be thrown into mouth of nests. After wasps are dead, dig out nest and destroy grubs.

WEED-KILLER : (See *Sulphuric Acid*.)

WHITE FLY : Serious pest of tomato and other indoor crops. Can be controlled by fumigation, using either hydrocyanic-acid gas or tetrachlorethane. Latter most commonly used as less dangerous. Supply of white fly parasite should be obtained to keep pest in check. Adult lays eggs in pupæ of pest, and grubs feed on them.

WIREWORMS : Many other soil insects are confused with this common pest. It is larval stage of click beetle and lives on roots and other underground parts of plants. Life as larva may be from three to five years. Eggs are laid mainly in grass ; hence land newly broken from turf is generally infested. Wireworms are easily recognised. Usually about ¾-in. long when full grown, yellowish-brown in colour and of rather shining appearance. Long and thin and tough-skinned. Head has pair of strong jaws. Three pairs of short legs behind head, and at other end of the body is small stub-like appendage known as the " anal-foot." Pest is not easy to control and is hard to destroy.

If land is carefully dug in winter and thrown up rough, birds will pick out many, and frost will kill others. If soil is badly infested, dressing of naphthalene, 3 ozs. per square yard, can be forked in during late winter. Also set traps, such as pieces of carrot or potato pushed below surface of soil, skewered on a piece of wood, to pull out easily. Examine frequently and destroy the wireworms attached.

WOODLICE : These creatures feed on plant refuse and frequently on living plants. Discouraged in garden and greenhouse by cleanliness and by removing rotting woodwork and rubbish. Dusting them and their haunts with pyrethrum powder is most effective method of reducing numbers.

WOOLLY APHIS : Serious pest of fruit trees, particularly apples. Also known as *American Blight*. Insects penetrate holes and cracks in bark, live on the sap, and cause scab-like swelling which is gradually extended. Tardistillate spraying kills some in autumn. Additional methods are to spray immediately after leaf fall with paraffin emulsion, and the woolly tufts can be brushed off with paraffin or methylated spirit in summer.

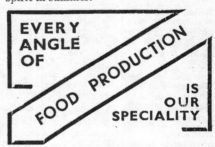
and failures, and avoid the same old mistakes year after year. ▶

Your Sowing & Planting Guide

SEED QUANTITY TABLE

VEGETABLE	SEED REQUIRED FOR A 50 FT. SOWING	VEGETABLE	SEED REQUIRED FOR A 50 FT. SOWING
Artichoke, Jerusalem...	6 lb.	Parsnip	$\frac{1}{4}$ oz.
Beans, Broad	(double row) 1 pt.	Pea	1 pt.
Beans, Dwarf	$\frac{1}{2}$ pt.	Potato (early) ...	7 lb.
Beans, Haricot ...	$\frac{1}{2}$ pt.	Potato (maincrop) ...	5 lb.
Beans, Runner... ...	(double row) 1 pt.	Radish	$\frac{3}{4}$ oz.
Beet	1 oz.	Spinach	$\frac{1}{2}$ oz.
Carrot	$\frac{1}{4}$ oz.	Spinach Beet ...	$\frac{1}{4}$ oz.
Lettuce	$\frac{1}{4}$ oz.	Turnip, Swede ...	$\frac{1}{4}$ oz.
Onion	$\frac{1}{2}$ oz.	Turnip	$\frac{1}{4}$ oz.
Parsley	$\frac{1}{4}$ oz.	Vegetable Marrow ...	(3 per station) 36 seeds

SEEDS SOWN UNDER GLASS OR IN SEED BED

VEGETABLE	SEEDS TO SUPPLY 200 PLANTS	VEGETABLE	SEEDS TO SUPPLY 200 PLANTS
*Broccoli	$\frac{1}{8}$ oz.	*Lettuce	$\frac{1}{8}$ oz.
*Brussels Sprouts	$\frac{1}{8}$ oz.	Onion	$\frac{1}{4}$ oz.
*Cabbage	$\frac{1}{8}$ oz.	Tomato	225 seeds
*Cauliflower	$\frac{1}{8}$ oz.	Vegetable Marrow	210 seeds
Leek	$\frac{1}{4}$ oz.		

** A normal small packet will supply enough plants for the average garden or allotment.*

YOUR PLANTING AND SOWING TABLE

CROP	TIME TO SOW IN THE OPEN	TIME TO PLANT	DISTANCE BETWEEN PLANTS	DISTANCE BETWEEN ROWS	PERIOD OF USE
Artichoke Jerusalem ...	—	March	12 in.	3 ft.	Nov.–March
Beans, Broad ...	Nov.–April	Mar.–April	6–9 in.	2 ft.	June–Aug.
Beans, Dwarf ...	May–July	May–June	6–9 in.	18 in.–2 ft.	July–Sept.
Beans, Haricot ...	May–July	May	6–9 in.	18 in.–2 ft.	Winter
Beans, Runner ...	May–June	May–June	12 in.	6 ft.	July–Sept.
Beet	April–July	—	6–9 in.	12 in.	All year
Broccoli	April–May	May–July	18–24 in.	$1\frac{1}{2}$–2 ft.	Oct.–May
Broccoli, Sprouting	April	June–July	2 ft.	2 ft.	Winter
Brussels Sprouts ...	Mar.–April	May–June	2–3 ft.	2–3 ft.	Winter
Cabbage	March–May	April–July	12–24 in.	$1\frac{1}{2}$–2 ft.	June–Dec.
Carrot	April–July	—	6–9 in.	12 in.	All year
Cauliflower ...	April–May	April–July	18–24 in.	$1\frac{1}{2}$–2 ft.	May–Oct.
Kale	April	June–July	2 ft.	2 ft.	Winter
Leeks	March	April–June	6 in.	12 in.	Winter
Lettuce	March–July	April–June	6–9 in.	12 in.	Summer
Marrow	May	May–June	2 ft.	4 ft.	June–Oct.
Onions	March	April–May	6–9 in.	12 in.	Winter
Onions, Salad ...	April–June	—	Close	9 in.	June–Sept.
Parsnips	Feb.–March	—	9 in.	15–18 in.	Winter
Peas, Dwarf ...	March–July	—	2–3 in.	2 ft.	June–Oct.
Peas, Tall ...	April–June	—	2–3 in.	4–6 ft.	July–Sept.
Radish	April–Aug.	—	Close	6 in.	Summer
Savoy	April–May	May–July	12–24 in.	$1\frac{1}{2}$–2 ft.	Aug.–March
Shallots	—	Feb.–March	6–9 in.	12 in.	July onwards
Spinach	March–July	—	6–9 in.	12 in.	Summer
Spinach Beet ...	April–July	—	9 in.	12–15 in.	July–March
Swedes	April–June	—	9 in.	15 in.	Oct.–April
Tomato	—	June	15–18 in.	3 ft.	Aug.–Oct.
Turnips	April–July	—	6–9 in.	12 in.	May–Dec.

Printed by TEE & WHITEN and J. MEAD LTD., 21, CITY ROAD, LONDON, E.C.1.

Vim and Vigour on the VEGETABLE FRONT

Here we come, fine specimens all, as healthy as healthy can be. We've been fed on soil enriched with the finest Fertilizer you can find. Victory Vegetables—that's what we are.

CLAY'S FERTILIZER

The Guarantor— of CROPS Galore

Sold everywhere in branded and sealed bags : 7 lbs. 3/9 ; 14 lbs. 6/3 ; 28 lbs. 10/6 ; 56 lbs. 19/- ; 112 lbs. 34/-.

CLAY & SON, LTD., STRATFORD, LONDON, E.15